BARNES WALLIS
DAMBUSTER

BARNES WALLIS

DAMBUSTER

PETER PUGH

ICON BOOKS

Published in the UK in 2005 by
Icon Books Ltd, The Old Dairy,
Brook Road, Thriplow,
Cambridge SG8 7RG
email: info@iconbooks.co.uk
www.iconbooks.co.uk

Sold in the UK, Europe, South Africa and Asia
by Faber and Faber Ltd, 3 Queen Square,
London WC1N 3AU
or their agents

Distributed in the UK, Europe, South Africa and Asia
by TBS Ltd, Frating Distribution Centre, Colchester Road,
Frating Green, Colchester CO7 7DW

Published in Australia in 2005
by Allen and Unwin Pty Ltd,
PO Box 8500, 83 Alexander Street,
Crows Nest, NSW 2065

Distributed in Canada by
Penguin Books Canada,
90 Eglinton Avenue East, Suite 700,
Toronto, Ontario M4P 2YE

ISBN 1 84046 685 5

Typesetting by Hands Fotoset

Printed and bound in the UK by Cromwell Press Ltd.

Contents

CONTENTS

CONTENTS

LIST OF ILLUSTRATIONS

ACKNOWLEDGEMENTS

No book is ever written without the help of a number of people. In writing about Barnes Wallis I have called on those books already written by others, notably the one previous biography by Jack Morpurgo, published in 1972. Other books and papers on which I have drawn can be seen in the Bibliography at the end of this book. At Icon Books, the typing of the manuscript has been done by Betty Thompson and the editing by Ruth Tidball.

For photographs I have relied on the Cambridge University Library and the Imperial War Museum.

THE VALUE OF MONEY

In a book about business we cannot ignore the changing value of money, and – with the exception of the inter-war years – the 20th century was inflationary. There is no magic formula for translating 1900 prices into those of 2005. Some items have exploded in price, others have declined. We have to choose some criterion of measurement, and I have chosen the average working wage.

The Victorian age was one of stable prices, but they started to rise just before the First World War, and rose sharply at the end of it. (Wars are always inflationary, because they distort supply and demand.) Immediately after the war, prices were more than twice as high as in 1914, and although they declined somewhat in the depressed economic conditions of the 1920s and 30s, they remained about twice as high as those before the war.

Price controls and rationing were imposed in the Second World War, but as these were withdrawn, prices again doubled. Inflation continued at about 3 per cent a year through the 1950s and 60s, but then rose sharply, almost catastrophically, in the 1970s. Although it was brought under control by the end of that decade, there were two more nasty upward blips in the early and late 1980s before the more stable 1990s and early years of the 21st century.

I have used the following formula:

Late 19th century – multiply by 115 to equate with today's prices
Early 20th century – multiply by 110 to equate with today's prices
1918–45 – multiply by 55 to equate with today's prices
1945–50 – multiply by 30 to equate with today's prices
1950–60 – multiply by 25 to equate with today's prices
1960–70 – multiply by 20 to equate with today's prices
1970–74 – multiply by 16 to equate with today's prices
1975–77 – multiply by 11 to equate with today's prices
1978–80 – multiply by 7 to equate with today's prices
1980–87 – multiply by 4 to equate with today's prices
1987–91 – multiply by 2 to equate with today's prices
1991–97 – multiply by 1.5 to equate with today's prices

Since 1997, the rate of inflation, by the standards of most of the 20th century, has been very low, averaging less than the Labour government's originally stated aim of 2.5 per cent (since reduced to 2 per cent). You don't need me to tell you that some things, such as telephone charges and many items made in the Far East, notably China, are going down in price, while others, such as houses, have moved up very sharply.

INTRODUCTION

When I was an undergraduate at Churchill College, Cambridge, in the early 1960s I went to a lecture in the Churchill College Hall by the great man Barnes Wallis (still not knighted at that stage). It was not long after the release of the hugely popular film *The Dambusters*, and Wallis was a national hero. The Hall was packed, and I could only secure a seat right at the back. I retain this memory of a small, white-haired man seen at a distance. However, I also have the memory of his telling us that we would soon be flying to Australia in two-and-a-half hours because an aircraft which he was developing would fly to a great height and then cross to Australia at hypersonic speed. As we know, the flight still takes nearly 24 hours, though I still think it's wonderful that I can leave cold and dank England in late February and 24 hours later be in Melbourne watching the first Formula One Grand Prix of the year in the lovely sun-drenched Albert Park. Maybe my grandchildren will do the journey in Wallis's two-and-a-half hours.

I think this story about Wallis encapsulates him, for he was a man of vision and seemed to spend most of his life persuading, and often arguing with, those who did not quite share his vision. Like many visionaries he was convinced that people were trying to obstruct him deliberately. In this he was very like his contemporary Frank Whittle, and in both cases they were largely wrong. Most people were only too keen to help them, but in many cases those who seemed obstructive were merely facing up to the reality that the technology needed to fulfil their dreams was not yet ready and needed to be developed.

Wallis is, of course, best known for his 'bouncing bombs'. Indeed, this idea was truly bold, and the feat which 617 Squadron, led by the brave Guy Gibson, achieved in breaching the Möhne and Eder dams was a remarkable one. There have been many arguments for and against in assessing whether the destruction and disruption wrought by the attacks was worth all the effort and the aircraft and airmen lost, but there can be no gainsaying the favourable effect on the morale of the British and the occupied peoples of Europe.

However, as we shall see, Barnes Wallis is more than bouncing bombs. He made significant contributions in other fields of aircraft engineering, first in airships and then in a revolutionary way of constructing aircraft, most notably used in the Wellesley and Wellington bombers. His views on how best to make bombing effective – by using heavy, earth-shattering bombs – were finally adopted by the powers-that-be and proved their efficacy immediately.

Unfortunately, his final project – variable geometry aircraft – suffered from a lack of funds and commitment, largely because Britain's reduced economic circumstances meant that the country could not afford every new military project put forward. Nevertheless, when he died in 1979, at the age of 92, Wallis could look back on a life of great endeavour and achievement.

Peter Pugh, June 2005

Chapter One

He Used Science to Teach Us to Think

ALWAYS SHORT OF MONEY

Barnes Neville Wallis was born in Ripley, Derbyshire, on 26 September 1887, the second son of Charles and Edith Wallis. Queen Victoria had already been on the throne for 50 years and would reign for another fourteen. It was the height of the age when Great Britain's navy ruled the seas and everyone knew what the 'Great' meant. The reality for most of the British population, though, was a life of unremitting struggle, and it was not easy for the Wallis family. Barnes's father Charles had come down from Oxford wanting to be a doctor, and after four years of study had made the grade. However, to find a practice he had been forced to move north to Ripley, where his shy manner was interpreted by many as arrogance. The coterie of patients, never large, dwindled and in 1891 the Wallises fled back to Woolwich in London, where their families lived and where they had first met. They were extremely short of money (Barnes's enduring memory of his parents was that they were *always* short of money). Nevertheless, appearances had to be maintained if Charles was going to be a successful doctor. The house where the Wallis family lived, 241 New Cross Road, was large, and a live-in maid was employed at £5 a year plus keep, as well as a nanny and an errand boy to deliver the medicines.

Barnes's mother Edith, in spite of their parlous financial position, was determined that her sons be properly educated, and this meant attendance at what the British call a 'public' school. To the rest of the world it means a 'private' school.

How would the Wallis family achieve this? The answer was Christ's Hospital (not a hospital but a school). Most public schools educate those who can afford their fees. Christ's Hospital educates only the poor, and the boys are taught, housed and fed for nothing. Furthermore, the school often pays the university fees of some of its pupils. But of course, the school does not take *any* boy just because he is poor. The boy must demonstrate ability and must be nominated by a Governor. Fortunately, Barnes Wallis was able to achieve both.

Once at the school, Wallis was extremely lucky to be taught by Henry Armstrong and Charles E. Browne. Armstrong was an internationally renowned chemist and was responsible for bringing method into the teaching of science, not only at Christ's Hospital but in public schools in general. Browne, selected by Armstrong to succeed him at Christ's, exercised an enormous influence on Wallis, as well as on a number of others – five of his boys were elected Fellows of the Royal Society.

Wallis wrote of Chas. Browne:

Tall and spare in build, with fair hair and moustache and healthy pallor of complexion, striding swiftly along, his gown billowing out behind him in the wind of his own progress. But, once in the laboratory, all the haste and energy of physical motion were replaced by a serene calm that could only come from the deepest confidence in and love for the thing he had to do. I never heard Uncle Chas. raise his voice; I never knew him give any punishment; I never knew him answer a question save by another; if necessary question after question, each framed with a skill amounting to inspiration, until the laggard brain of his pupil did at last see light. Uncle Chas. (as he came affectionately to be called) did not teach science in the sense usually attached to the word; he used science to teach us to think, to reveal to us the powers we ourselves possessed.

The top prize at the school was the Wilcox Prize. Wallis won it (he also came top in German, so he won the Form Prize as well). Sixty-four years later, Wallis wrote: 'My one asset is that I was taught to *think* by Uncle Chas.'

IT HAS TO BE ENGINEERING

In spite of this success, Wallis did not go to university, and indeed he left Christ's without any qualification at the age of eighteen. He could have gone into the City, where there were many fellow-Blues from school. However, he decided he wanted to be an engineer. The family had no contacts in this industry, and for weeks Wallis and his father (now severely handicapped after contracting poliomyelitis) tramped from engineering works to engineering works. Finally, they found him a place at Thames Engineering at the foot of Blackheath Hill at the princely wage of four shillings a week (20p, or £22 in today's money).

The future for marine engineering was bright. The arms race with Germany had begun following the German Navy Acts of 1895 and 1902. The British government propounded the policy – never achieved – of laying down two keels for every German one. There would be plenty of work for marine engineers. However, the Thames was not the place to be. The last battleship to be built on the Thames, *The Black Prince*, was already nearing completion. The Thames Engineering Company was struggling and tried diversification; for example, Wallis found himself working on the first racing-car built in England and on the prototype London taxi cab.

Wallis could see that he would have to move and, using the influence of his uncle, who had been an electrical engineer, in 1908 he moved to John Samuel Wright's shipyard at Cowes on the Isle of Wight. At Wright's, Wallis progressed to the drawing board and became friends with H.B. Pratt, who sat at the next board. Pratt had been involved in the early construction of airships at the great armaments manufacturer Vickers. Airships were to play a very significant role in Wallis's life for the next twenty years, so we need to look at the background to their development.

MAYFLY BUT IT NEVER DID

In 1884, three years before Wallis was born, two French army officers had achieved powered flight in their non-rigid airship, *La France*. They reached 12,000 feet and a speed of about 20 mph. In 1898 Count von Zeppelin, after a distinguished career as a cavalry officer, retired from the army and formed a company to build rigid airships, and on 2 July 1900 the first Zeppelin, no less than 420 feet in length, stayed in the air for eight hours and flew 211 miles. The fourth Zeppelin crossed the Alps. As the competition between the navies of Britain and Germany intensified during the first decade of the new century, realisation came to the British government that in terms of air power Germany was years ahead. The government turned to the leading arms company, Vickers, and in the 1909–10 Naval Estimates there was included a sum of £35,000 (about £4 million today) for His Majesty's Airship Number 1. Those given the task at Vickers had no experience whatsoever (they even indulged in some amateur espionage at Zeppelin's works in Friedrichshaven), and it soon became clear that this project was going to take some time.

Conceived in the fertile mind of Captain R.H.S. Bacon, Director of Naval Ordnance, blessed by the new Committee of Imperial Defence, watched over by a special group of officers detailed by the Admiralty, and given the Cavendish Dock at Barrow, the project looked hopeful. However, it was doomed by lack of experience. The airship was to be big: 512 feet in length with a diameter of 48 feet and a gas capacity of 640,000 cubic feet. She was to have a speed of 40 knots over 24 hours, be able to climb to 15,000 feet and have powerful (and therefore heavy) wireless apparatus. This meant that if she came down at sea she could be rescued. Finally, the Admiralty wanted her to be able to operate in the Arctic.

Progress was slow. The official history of Vickers by J.D. Scott was scathing:

The framework of the airship was to be constructed of Duralumin, an aluminium alloy which had been patented in 1905 by the German Conrad Claussen, and of which Vickers were, in 1910, to buy the patent rights. Being a new material, Duralumin was not very easy to deal with.

The No. 1 Rigid Naval Airship progressed slowly. Conceived in May, she was called the *Mayfly*, and as time went by there were jokes about her delayed emergence from the chrysalis. Nor did the designers or builders get from their masters the support to which they were entitled. While the airship was under construction Captain Sueter 'received more than one letter from the Controller of the Navy, saying high authority at the Admiralty did not believe in airships'. Thus encouraged, the designers not unnaturally modified, remodified and modified again. More and more weight was added in an attempt to meet the different requirements, until Robertson became anxious, and decided to lighten the ship by removing some of the structure, including the main keel member. One of his assistants, H.B. Pratt, who had mathematics adequate to the task, calculated that in this condition the ship would break up. But his calculations were not accepted. It was two years before the *Mayfly* at last left the hangar.

For a moment at any rate the doubters were silenced. The *Mayfly* was the largest airship which anyone had ever seen, and as she emerged from her shed in the Cavendish Dock at Barrow, she was a beautiful and impressive sight. For four days she was moored at her mast in Cavendish Dock, beaten by a forty-mile-an-hour wind. It was a trial of strength which she survived; but strength involves weight, and her lifting power (never large in any airship and requiring great experience to calculate) even now was not enough. The men got her back into the hangar; she was modified and appeared again in September. The airship shed was very narrow, and getting the airship out 'was like drawing a cork out of a bottle'. Caught in another gust of wind, the *Mayfly* broke her back. She was never rebuilt.

However, one man emerged from the disaster with his reputation enhanced. H.B. Pratt, then a junior draughtsman at Vickers' Barrow shipyard, though not on the *Mayfly* team, had written a paper explaining why it would never fly. Being right did not endear Pratt to his supervisors, and when he refused to sign a five-year personal commitment in 1912, Vickers let him go. He moved to John Samuel Wright and found himself next to Barnes Wallis.

In spite of Vickers' initial failure with *Mayfly*, the company was instructed by the government to try again (early in 1913 the German government had placed an order for ten Zeppelins). The Managing Director of Vickers, Sir Trevor Dawson, remembered Pratt's paper and told his subordinates to find him and bring him back to Vickers as Chief Draughtsman, Airships. Pratt returned, and within weeks asked Wallis to join him as Chief Assistant on the designing of the '*Zeppelin* larger than any yet made'. Wallis had now progressed to a salary of £3.5s.0d a week (£3.25, or £360 in today's money).

Pratt and Wallis did not work at Barrow, but rented a flat in Victoria Street, London, in the name of Mountain. This was to fool any German spy who might be interested in their work. In reality, the spying was likely to be all the other way, and indeed, in late 1913 they secured some valuable information on the Zeppelin by courtesy of Britain's new ally, the French.

In April 1913, the Germans' latest Zeppelin had made a forced landing on a French army parade ground. The crew were lavishly entertained while French airship experts, photographers and even the Assistant Naval and Military Attachés from the British Embassy in Paris were brought in to study the airship. The dossier on *LZ.216* arrived at Mr Mountain's in Victoria Street in November 1913.

As well as this information surreptitiously acquired, more came quite openly from Germany through the purchase by Winston Churchill, First Lord of the Admiralty, of non-rigid airships from the Parseval Company in Berlin. Right up to the outbreak of war in August 1914, the Parseval engineers were passing information to Pratt.

In spite of all this enthusiasm for airships, politics at the highest level meant that in the early months of the war the project was abandoned, and Wallis, for the second time in a few months (his first attempt had been stopped by Pratt), found himself applying for a post in the army. He enlisted in the Artists' Rifles, which Pratt had already joined. And there they would have stayed and, in all likelihood, been killed at the Front, if politics had not intervened again.

On 19 May 1915 a coalition government was formed, and though Winston Churchill fought hard to keep his job at the Admiralty, he was replaced by A.J. Balfour, the former Conservative Prime Minister, and was given the Duchy of Lancaster. Balfour decided that the construction of airships should be reviewed. Corporals Pratt and Wallis were found and transferred from the Artists' Rifles to become Sub-Lieutenants H.B. Pratt and B.N. Wallis in Her Majesty's Royal Navy.

Their lives were still dogged by indecision and political fighting, and it was not until 1917 that real progress on a workable airship design was made. Wallis had begun to work increasingly with Commander E.A.D. Masterman, who had been involved in the pre-war Vickers project. Masterman had appreciated, as had many others, that the existing methods of mooring and handling the airships on the ground were cumbersome. He and Wallis worked towards a more efficient mooring mast system. They wanted the airship to be able to attach herself to her mooring without landing first, with a minimum of outside assistance and in all weathers. Gassing and fuelling would have to be practical and rapid, and finally and perhaps most importantly, the airship should be able to fly off direct from her mooring.

Although Pratt, general manager of Vickers' airship project, had clearly been the senior of the two, Wallis's engineering brain, his ability to absorb detail and his vision moved him up alongside Pratt in his value to the airship project.

THINK ATLANTIC

Masterman had also sent a paper round Whitehall in September 1917 suggesting a new strategic role for airships.

In his view, the Navy should lose its obsession with the North Sea and think about convoy protection in the Atlantic. The Royal Navy were convinced that the danger came from the German navy based across the North Sea. (After all, the only major naval engagement of the First World War was the Battle of Jutland.) This would mean a smaller, stronger, faster and more manoeuvrable airship. The Admiralty agreed, and Vickers was instructed to build the R80.

Delighted at this turn of events, Wallis prepared the specifications for the R80 in less than two months. It would be a ship of only 1,200,000 cubic feet and would achieve a speed faster than any airship in existence. Her parts would be standardised, thereby reducing her building cost. Gondolas and hull would be streamlined. He also planned to reduce the weight of the cars to 50 per cent of that of the latest Zeppelins. The R80 would have four 230 hp Wolseley-Maybach engines, would travel at up to 60 mph and maintain an average of 50 mph for almost 4,000 miles. Within a week of receiving Wallis's drawings, the Admiralty gave the order to Vickers to build a prototype, and within a month ordered a second ship, the R81.

In retrospect, it is easy to see that Wallis was not pursuing the most promising avenue in air travel. It was not, of course, so obvious at the time, as is shown by this Vickers memorandum of 1918:

The outstanding and peculiar advantage of the Airship for Air Transport is its capacity for making non-stop voyages of long duration; whereas from inherent limitations, the Aeroplane will probably never, unless some radically new principle of design is discovered – be capable of carrying a passenger load for greater non-stop distances than 2,000 miles, and for economical operation, will probably be never used for non-stop flights of more than 1,000; whereas on the other hand, the only limit to the non-stop length of flight that can be made by an Airship is determined by the size of the ship, and 10,000 miles is quite practicable.

J.E. (Jack) Morpurgo put it succinctly in his book *Barnes Wallis* (published in 1972):

[Wallis] missed the logic of his own arguments as they might have applied to his own career.

There were other and substantial signposts, but all of them he failed to read: by 1918 aeroplanes were achieving speeds of 150 mph and could climb to 24,000 feet. At the end of the war bombers such as Germany's Gotha could carry a load of sixteen 112-lb bombs and sustain 80 mph for eight hours. There were in Britain over 3,000 first-line planes in service and 350,000 men and women employed in the aircraft industry. In comparison with this vast development and substantial improvement the British programme of rigid airship construction had proved ineffectual.

However, in 1918 and 1919 Wallis was not contemplating the relative failure of airships. He was working flat-out, developing his plans for the R80 and for the Masterman-Wallis mooring gear. By the time the R80

11

began trials she was even faster than Wallis had expected, and also some two tons lighter.

Harald Penrose, in his *British Aviation, The Adventuring Years 1920–1929*, wrote:

> For a moment airships held the scene. At last the Vickers-built R.80 had been brought from her shed and given her first trial on 19 July. The most streamlined British airship so far built, her length was 530 feet with diameter of 70 feet and capacity of 1,250,000 cubic feet affording a total lift of 38.5 tons and disposable load of 17.5 tons; maximum speed was 65 mph with a cruising radius of 6,500 miles.

Earlier, in March 1919, H.B. Pratt had written to his director, Sir James McKechnie, saying:

> In considering the subject of international mail services the most experienced technical staff should at once be engaged for airships under a technical chief who has the confidence of the British Government.

Pratt meant Barnes Wallis. Furthermore, he proposed to the Vickers Chairman, Sir Trevor Dawson, that:

> For the summer of 1920 I suggest we run sightseeing tours around the battlefields using R80 which could carry 80, each making three trips a week.

He had also investigated the possibility of using the big British airships and the recently acquired Zeppelins on flights between Cairo and Karachi and eventually to Australia.

However, the Chief of the Air Staff announced in January 1921 that R80 was of no further use to the nation. Disillusioned, Wallis offered his services to the American Commander J.C. Humaker of the US Navy, who Wallis knew greatly admired his work on the R80. It was true that the US Navy had plans for enlarging its airship arm, but Humaker feared nothing would come of them. He wrote to Wallis:

> There is great political agitation directed against the expenditure of money on naval expansion and while the argument is going on heavily, the matter of funds is held in abeyance. As things stand now it appears to be unlikely that authority can be obtained to build or acquire any additional rigid airship.

Vickers closed its Airship Department, moved most of the department's employees to other areas, and asked Wallis to carry on 'thinking about' airships while continuing to pay him £250 a year (£13,750 today). However, in December 1921 he received a letter from Vickers giving him less than one month's notice but taking 'the opportunity of thanking you for your loyal and efficient service to the company'.

Wallis, though by this time in his early 30s, took the opportunity to gain a degree, and applied for a job teaching Mathematics to School Certificate level at Chillon College, an English-type public school in Switzerland. He was accepted at a salary of £220 (£12,000). In spite of this radical change in his career, Wallis did not abandon all hope of resuming work on airships – by this time he was, after all, the country's foremost expert. And his chance to return to his love came through a Commander Dennistoun Burney. During the war, Burney had invented the Paravene, a device for cutting mines adrift from their moorings at sea. Burney earned a great deal in royalties from this device, and had also arranged to have an office inside the manufacturer of the Paravene, Vickers.

THE R100

Burney became convinced that the most efficient way to fly to the far-flung parts of the British Empire was by airship. Conversations in Germany with Zeppelin's successor, Dr Hugo Eckener, only served to reinforce his view. Burney pushed his ideas as far as the Air Council. Eventually he received government approval for his scheme and he put together a small team, inviting Wallis to be the Secretary to the committee. He added that the Secretary was really the most powerful member, because he was 'in a position to manipulate the minutes thereof in any way that he, the Secretary wishes'.

Wallis thought about the offer and considered the other members of the committee, and turned Burney down. He would accept only if given sole charge of the design. He told Harald Penrose that Major Scott, the airship commander, a Major Colmore, a Lieutenant Commander in the Royal Navy, and Colonel Vincent 'Dopey' Richmond had all approached Burney with a view to being involved. He said:

When Burney told me of this, I refused to join in, for I considered that Colmore and Richmond knew nothing about actual design. I therefore schematically designed a suitable airship at home, showed it to Burney, who was sufficiently convinced to go ahead and persuaded Vickers to purchase the empty Howden shed and proceed on their own. The Airship Guarantee Company was formed 29 November 1923, the directors being Sir Trevor Dawson, Sir Vincent Caillard, Mr A. Cartwright, Commander Craven, and Lieutenant Commander C.D. Burney. H.B. Pratt who had been general manager in charge of Vickers war-time airship construction was no longer interested, and I, as his ex-chief designer, was appointed chief engineer.

Still there were many ups and downs before Wallis could really begin work on the new R100, but in the last months of 1924 he was able to do so. He designed an airship that would carry, in peacetime, 140 passengers at 90 mph with seven tons of luggage and another seven tons of mail for a distance of 3,761 miles. Flying at the lower speed of 72 mph, the range would be no less than 6,017 miles. In wartime, loaded with 20 tons of bombs, she could fly at 90 mph for a distance of 4,473 miles. Finally, as a naval reconnaissance vessel without any load, the R100 could fly at 56.7 mph to a distance of 17,890 miles – in other words, to go anywhere in the world. And, regardless of the weather, she would be able to start and end her journeys from a mast 170 feet high.

Wallis had considerable experience of working on airships, but the rest of the team were novices. His immediate assistant was Nevil Shute-Norway (known in the two decades following the Second World War as the novelist Nevil Shute, who enjoyed huge worldwide success with such novels as *No Highway*, *A Town like Alice* and *On the Beach*). Shute also wrote an autobiography, *Slide Rule*, in which he talked of his and Wallis's work on the R100:

> There was a great deal to be done before we dared to begin on the working drawings for the airship, and we had little past experience to guide us. Wallis was a veteran designer of the Vickers airships of the war years, but few of the rest of us had ever seen any airships, much less flown in one. From the start it was evident that it would be necessary to depart entirely from the Zeppelin design since this ship was to be more than twice the size of any airship that had flown before.
>
> The airship was to be built in East Yorkshire at Howden, a small town halfway between York and Hull. The aerodrome and its shed had not been used since 1921. Improvements in the mooring mast and the gasbag material were deemed essential and a new design for the girders was developed while new machines were produced to manufacture the helically-wound four-inch duralumin tubes of which the girders were to be built.

There were many difficulties, one of them being vertigo. Shute wrote that:

> When we first arrived at Howden I can very well remember venturing up the stairs to the passage ways in the roof of the shed a hundred and seventy feet above the concrete floor, petrified with fear and

clinging to the hand rails with sweating hands at every step. I remember, sick with fright, watching the riggers clambering about on the first frame to be hoisted, carrying out their work a hundred feet from the floor with the girders swaying and waving at each movement that they made.

Heating the shed was impossible and humidity both in summer and winter caused corrosion. Wallis was forced to instruct the builders of the airship to revarnish every girder by hand. It took 30 men three months and added a ton to the tare weight. Labour, too, was a problem in such a remote spot. Shute recalled that:

> We employed a large percentage of our labour in the form of local lads and girls straight off the farms as unskilled labour, training them to do simple riveting and mass production work. The lads were what one would expect, straight from the plough, but the girls were an eye-opener. They were brutish and uncouth, filthy in appearance and habits ... these girls straight off the farms were the lowest types that I have ever seen in England, and incredibly foul-mouthed. We very soon found that we had to employ a welfare worker to look after them because promiscuous intercourse was going on merrily in every dark corner.

At the same time as the privately-financed R100 was being built at Howden, a government-backed airship, named the R101, was being built at Cardington in Bedfordshire. The announcement ran:

17

The Government proposes to begin research and experiments at Cardington. We will first recondition one of the existing ships for research, and at an early date will proceed with building a new airship of 5,000,000 cubic feet capacity. We will construct the necessary intermediate and terminal bases overseas to enable two airships – one built by the Government and the other by contractors – to fly with safety between here and India. The contract for the second airship is ready for signature as soon as the House agrees. The total cost is £350,000 [about £19 million today]. The whole scheme involves a three-year programme and gross expenditure of £1,350,000 [£74 million]. The question of technical staff and of expert research workers has been fully explored, and the Ministry is satisfied that we are properly and fully equipped. We are looking for successful achievement in opening up a new era in Dominion relationship; with airships, communications between our blood relations overseas can be put on a closer basis than ever before.

Whereas expenditure on the R100 was carefully controlled, there seemed to be no limit on what could be spent on research and development at Cardington. However, whereas the R100 developers could rapidly change their minds if circumstances demanded it, the R101 designers were much less flexible – if public money had been spent on a development, into the ship it must go.

A glaring example of this different approach was in the engine. At Howden they experimented with using diesel engines but abandoned them, mainly because of the weight. Rolls-Royce Condor engines were installed instead. At Cardington, even though the designer also urged a switch to petrol engines, a Whitehall civil servant refused to authorise the switch and the R101 flew with overweight diesel engines.

In spite of all the difficulties, by the early summer of 1929, R100 was nearing completion and ready to have her gasbags inflated with hydrogen. The volume was no less than 5,000,000 cubic feet, giving the airship a gross lift of about 156 tons. Her tare weight was 102 tons, leaving 54 tons for fuel, ballast, crew and passengers. There were fourteen gasbags, and guiding them into place was no easy task. Shute wrote about the trickiness of the installation:

> The gasbags were inflated and hung in position by the design staff. I took one squad of riggers on to the girders of the ship and the chief draughtsman took another squad; the operation was directed by B.N. Wallis talking to us through a megaphone. This unconventional teamwork answered admirably and was much admired by a representative of the Zeppelin company who happened to be with us at the time, and to whom an office worker was an office worker, and a foreman a foreman. He had never seen anything like that in Germany. Neither had we in England, but it worked. All 14 gasbags were positioned in the ship after a fortnight's sweat and toil with only one small tear.

Then there were the engine trials, which were carried out successfully, though not without considerable anxiety.

Shute remembered that

> If a propeller had hit the floor or a suspension cable
> had parted under that test the issue could only have
> been sheer disaster and the loss of many lives.

Meanwhile the public were being conditioned on the
viability of airships. Wallis came down to London from
the remote Howden to lecture at the Royal Society of
Arts in May 1929. He disclosed some of the secrets of his
design, such as the spiral mesh net for the gasbags and the
method of making large tubes for the framework from
strips wound spirally and riveted. He told his audience:

> There are only 42 dissimilar components in the
> entire 730 foot structure; apart from variations in
> the thickness of metal, every girder is made from
> only seven of them; thus we could order items in lots
> of half millions, and make even only one airship a
> mass-production job. Despite initial anxiety in
> attaining the necessary accuracy we got the main
> girders, each 43 feet in length, within limits of plus
> or minus .01 inch.

As the R100 prepared for its flight, Shute reflected on
those involved:

> My chief was B.N. Wallis whose title was Chief
> Engineer. To my mind Wallis was the greatest
> engineer in England at that time and for 20 years
> afterwards. It was an education and a privilege to
> work under him, and I count myself lucky to have
> done so.

Shute also thought that Sir Dennistoun Burney, the Managing Director, was an outstanding and visionary leader. In Shute's view, Wallis's and Burney's talents were complementary, and fused to bring about the successful completion of the R100. Unfortunately, Wallis and Burney could not get on with each other and, as we shall see, once Wallis's design work was complete he gradually moved on to work on conventional aircraft.

In the event, the rival R101 flew on 14 October 1929, before the R100, whose developers learnt much about her from the press releases, most notably that her gross lift was 148 tons while her tare weight was 113 tons, leaving only 35 tons for the fuel, ballast, crew and passengers, compared with the 54 tons of the R100. In the view of those at Howden, the R101 was dangerously overweight and underpowered.

The R100 trial flight to Canada took place in the summer of 1930. This is how Shute recorded the landing at Montreal:

We moored to the mast at St Hubert airport at dawn, 78 hours out from Cardington [the R100 had been moved from Howden to Cardington for this epic flight]; we had five tons of fuel left. The great circle distance is about 3,300 land miles, so we had averaged about 42 mph. It must be remembered that at that time only one aeroplane had made a direct flight across the Atlantic from East to West against the prevailing wind, starting from Ireland and crashing on an island off the coast of Newfoundland at the very limit of its fuel, so that our performance, being twice the speed of ship and

21

trains from London to Montreal, gave some commercial promise.

After twelve days, R100 returned to Cardington. Meanwhile, R101 prepared for its first big flight – to India. It ended in disaster, with the airship crashing at Beauvais in France. Of 54 people on board, only six survived, four of whom were engineers in power cars. R100 never flew again, thanks to the horrors of the R101 accident putting paid to all further development of airships.

Inevitably, there was a public inquiry, and the conclusion reached was that the disaster had been caused by a large rent suddenly occurring in one of the most forward gasbags. Shute thought that this was probably correct, but he mentioned a number of other factors – lack of sufficient test flights; the insistence of the Secretary of State for Air, Lord Thomson of Cardington, on flying without sufficient testing and in bad weather, in order to stick to his political timetable; lack of objective outside inspection of the airship; and the weight of the diesel engine.

Shute was very critical of the state, as opposed to the private, approach to business. Even as he began work on the privately financed R100, he wrote:

I spent many hours reading old reports and records to find what had previously been done in airship calculations, and when I came on the report of the R.38 accident enquiry I sat stunned, unable to believe the words I was reading. I had come from the hard commercial school of de Havillands where competence was the key to survival, and disaster might have meant the end of the company [as indeed the Comet disasters did in the 1950s] and unemployment for everyone concerned. It was inexpressibly shocking to find that before building the vast and costly structure of R.38, the civil servants concerned made no attempt to calculate the aerodynamic forces acting on the ship, and I remember going to one of my chiefs with the report and asking if this could possibly be true.

Not only did he confirm it, but he pointed out that no one had been sacked over it or even suffered censure. Indeed, he said, the same team of men had been entrusted with the construction of another airship, the R101, which was to be built by the Air Ministry in competition with our own ship, the R100.

Shute was also critical of the lack of co-operation between the private company building the R100 at Howden and the government-backed one at Cardington. He wrote in *Slide Rule*:

In the five years that elapsed before either airship flew, neither designer visited the other's Works, nor did they meet or correspond on common problems each had to solve. Each trod a parallel road alone, harassed and overworked. Towards the end I made contact with my opposite number, Dr Roxbee Cox, and visited Cardington to see their ship, but his chiefs prevented him from visiting Howden. If the Cabinet wanted competition they had it with a vengeance, but I would not say it was healthy.

J.D. Scott in his book on Vickers felt that Shute became a little obsessed with the inefficiencies automatically associated with state-run enterprises. He wrote:

> Nevil Shute drew general conclusions about the relative competence of public and private enterprise, conclusions which were confirmed by his subsequent experience, until they came to have the force of religious belief.
>
> He had held these beliefs for a long time when he wrote his autobiography, which he did not do until many years later, and it is not surprising if neither his views nor even his recollections are altogether shared by his one-time colleagues. They do not recall that there was coldness between Howden and Cardington, for instance. Wallis liked to work alone and felt no need to discuss his problems with the Cardington people; the Cardington team, whose leaders had worked with Wallis at Barrow during the war, understood this, and the result was that the leaders of both sides were personally friendly but not professionally intimate.

Whatever the reasons, the R101 accident meant the end of airship development in Britain. By the end of 1930, the worldwide Depression was taking hold and the British government was looking at every possible means of cutting back on expenditure. The accident provided one as far as airships were concerned. As Shute pointed out, the government made the right decision, if for the wrong reason:

The performance of the aeroplane was to increase
... greatly in the next few years. At the time it did not
seem possible that the cruising speed of an airship
could ever much exceed eighty miles an hour, for
various technical reasons. Developments of the
aeroplane were to make this speed seem trivial, but I
doubt if these developments were in sight at the end
of 1930. It was not until 1933 that the Douglas DC1
astonished the aeronautical world with the revolutionary design based on the new controllable
propeller, the retractable undercarriage and the new
conception of the use of flaps ... We could have
made a start with airships by about 1934, but it
would have been a dead-end venture, for the aeroplane would have put us out of business in a few
years.

Chapter Two

Bombers

GEODETIC CONSTRUCTION

One of the most important design innovations of the 1920s, and one which was to prove itself later on the Wellesley and then the Wellington, was geodetic construction. What is geodetic construction? Chaz Bowyer in his book *The Wellington Bomber* describes it:

Part of Wallis's legacy of experience with airship design had been his conviction of the efficacy of using the new light alloy metals introduced by industry in general for airship and now, aeroplane structures; primarily for their huge savings in weight of overall structure, but also as the basis for another avenue of personal research, geodesics. Put at its simplest definition, geodesics are the shortest distance between two points on any curved surface – derived from the 'great-circle' principle of mathematics utilised in trans-oceanic navigation. The basic application of geodesic principles to aircraft structural design was by no means new in 1930 when Wallis commenced serious investigation into the subject; a similar fuselage construction for a

French aircraft had been on public display at the Paris Salon in 1921, for merely one example of earlier application. Nevertheless, Barnes Wallis's eventual introduction of *overall* geodetic construction in airframes was undoubtedly a watershed in British construction methods. His aims were not only to provide substantial savings in overall weight, but also to eliminate unnecessary bulkheads, bracers, et al, thus, in effect, offering a self-stressing, hollow structure, having a load bearing safety factor figure virtually twice that of contemporary, traditional structural designs.

The first full step of geodetic construction used by Wallis was on the gasbag wiring of the R100.

Wallis had been in no doubt that the R100 would be a great success, but during 1927 he began to take an interest in other aircraft and started a correspondence with engineers at the Blackburn Aircraft Company. At the same time he was becoming very disillusioned with Burney, as did most who worked for him or with him. His interest bore fruit fortuitously when one of the many visitors to the R100's base at Howden was the new Chairman of Vickers Aviation and the Supermarine Company (acquired by Vickers in 1928), Sir Robert McLean.

McLean was a Scottish engineer who had made his name running the Indian State Railways. J.D. Scott described him in his Vickers history as

A man of granite integrity and austere independence of mind ... [He] accepted authority as something which his character was bound to bring him, and the loneliness of high responsibility as his natural habitat. Able subordinates he would treasure and protect to the utmost of his immense capacity; others did not survive.

McLean was noted for his skill in handling people. He soon appreciated the abilities of Wallis and decided that he wanted him in mainstream development of aircraft for Vickers. However, he appreciated that there was potential for friction between him and R.K. Pierson, the Chief Designer for Vickers Aviation. Pierson was one of the pioneer aircraft engineers, and had been the designer of the Vickers Vimy bombers of the First World War. And, of course, it was a Vimy that had been flown by Alcock and Brown in their record-breaking flight across the Atlantic in 1919. Pierson was a giant in the industry, very close to, and completely trusted by, the pilots of the war who were now senior members of the RAF, the biggest customer of Vickers Aviation.

McLean arranged for Pierson and his son to visit Wallis at Howden to look at the R100. Fortunately, Pierson and Wallis hit it off, and McLean invited Wallis to Vickers Aviation's headquarters at Weybridge and offered him the job of Chief Designer. He would form a triumvirate of Chief Designers, along with Pierson and Reginald Mitchell, the designer of the Supermarine S5 and S6 which won the Schneider Trophy for Britain – and the designer, in coming years, of the Spitfire.

McLean was lucky to have under him men of such talent. Indeed, two of them, Reginald Mitchell and Barnes Wallis, were so outstanding that the sobriquet 'genius' has often been applied to them. Finally, making up a quartet of brilliant and dedicated men, there was Mutt Summers, Vickers' chief test pilot.

Scott's view of how Wallis fitted into this group was as follows:

> Barnes Wallis's ruling passion, in heavier-than-air aircraft as it had been in airships, was the achievement of high-speed, long-range flight. To this object, he was prepared, now as in the design of the R100, and in the most literal sense of the term, to dedicate himself; in summoning Wallis to his side McLean had summoned a man whose austerity and independence were deeply sympathetic to his own. In the technique of design Wallis belonged to a later generation than Pierson, conversant with light alloys and the structures associated with them, and he understood the necessity of giving far longer periods of time to the design and development of new shapes of aircraft far more complex and sophisticated than the aircraft of the Twenties.

Wallis's integration into Vickers Aircraft was slow, as he was still involved with the R100 and its race with the government-backed R101. Before he could extricate himself completely from airships, Wallis had to suffer the humiliation of not being invited on the successful maiden flight of his R100 to Canada.

However, eventually he was able to concentrate on heavier-than-air aircraft and, after a disastrous spell trying to work with Mitchell at the Supermarine works at Southampton, became involved in solving a fuselage problem on a fighter designed by Pierson.

This is how Wallis described his relationships with Mitchell and Pierson:

Mitchell and I took alternate trains to London, he to tell the board that he would not have this fellow interfering with his work, and I telling them that I didn't think this was a practical suggestion.

When Pierson offered him a job at Weybridge, Barnes Wallis said he would take it only if he were equal in seniority to Pierson himself.

He was the most generous man I have ever known. Fancy having an interloper who did not know one end of an aeroplane from another coming in with equal status. But I did.

BOMBING

Now Wallis was in a position to concentrate on aeroplanes and, in view of the increasingly fraught atmosphere of the 1930s, it was bound to be bombers that Vickers wanted him to work on.

Before looking at his revolutionary work on bombers and bombs, we should consider the place of bombing in the thinking of both the leading politicians of the day and those at the top of the Royal Air Force.

The first bombing of the modern age took place at Liège in Belgium on 6 August 1914, two days after war was declared. A German Zeppelin killed nine civilians with its bombs. Britain's first attempt was not a success, although its target, the Zeppelin sheds at Cologne and

Düsseldorf, was at least a military one. In heavy mist, three of the four Royal Naval Air Service biplanes failed to find the target; the fourth dropped its bombs on Düsseldorf, but they did not explode.

Throughout the First World War, bombing by both sides was sporadic and, in the context of the wholesale slaughter of the trenches, largely irrelevant. Nevertheless, it gave a portent of the future. The debate about whether bombers should be built as a potential weapon, or whether fighters should be built as a defensive weapon, or indeed whether both should be banned in the interest of world peace, continued unabated through the 1920s into the 30s. Tempering the debate was a much-quoted remark by Conservative Prime Minister Stanley Baldwin, in a speech on 12 November 1932:

> I think it is well for the man in the street to realise that there is no power on earth that can protect him from being bombed. Whatever people may tell him, the bomber will always get through ... The only defence is in offence, which means that you have to kill more women and children more quickly than the enemy if you want to save yourselves.

Winston Churchill, former Conservative Chancellor of the Exchequer but by the early 1930s out of office, countered this comment by Baldwin with a different view:

> We may ourselves ... be confronted on some occasion with a visit from an ambassador, and may have to give an answer, and if that answer is not

satisfactory, within the next few hours the crash of bombs exploding in London ... will warn us of an inadequacy which has been permitted in our aerial defences.

Churchill said this to the House of Commons on 7 February 1934, and a month later Baldwin promised the House that 'in air strength and in air power this country shall no longer be in a position inferior to any country within striking distance of our shores'.

By the summer of 1934, the 'alphabet schemes' were being put in hand. Scheme A would produce 500 front-line bombers. By March 1935, Scheme C planned to double the number of bombers to be produced by March 1939 from 476 to 816 and, by the time Scheme H was put in place, the number was doubled again.

In March 1934, the British government, realising that the Disarmament Conference convened by the League of Nations was a sham (both Germany and Japan had given notice of their intention to quit the League), announced that Britain was to have parity with the German air force. Thereafter, the orders for more bombers under the 'alphabet' schemed markedly increased.

Sir Arthur 'Bomber' Harris, Marshal of the RAF during the Second World War, wrote in his *Bomber Offensive*, published in 1947:

It was the first defensive aspect of the air war of 1914–1918 that first brought the conception of an air force independent of the other two services, and of independent air operations. Daylight attacks on London by German aircraft in June and July of 1917 caused so much disturbance that General Smuts, then a member of the War Cabinet, was asked to get out a report on the whole subject. In this report he said that the air arm 'can be used as an independent means of war operations. Nobody who witnessed the attack on London on 11th July could have any doubt on this point ... As far as at present can be foreseen there is absolutely no limit to the scale of its future independent war use. And the day may not be far off when aerial operations with their devastation of enemy lands and destruction of industrial and populous centres on a vast scale may become the principal operations of war, to which the older forms of military and naval operations may become secondary and subordinate.

Harris certainly believed in the efficacy of bombing. He wrote after the war:

I certainly had faith in the bomber offensive – if it could be got going, and if the Germans did not find effective counter-measures before we had built up the force. The surest way to win a war is to destroy the enemy's war potential. And all that I had seen and studied of warfare in the past had led me to believe that the bomber was the predominant weapon for this task in this war.

Wallis's idea of a really big bomb, which will be discussed later, found a ready listener in 'Bomber' Harris, who had long since realised the limitations of using small, conventional bombs. He wrote in his *Bomber Offensive*:

Any one of the three classes of industrial target –
synthetic oil plants, aircraft factories and aluminium plants – attacked by Bomber Command in 1940
would, in the later stages of the war, have had to
be given first priority for attack by both Bomber
Command and the USAAF for a considerable period
if a campaign against them was to have any chance
of success. But in 1940, besides these industrial
targets, we were also required to bomb German
communications, both railways and canals, in the
area of the Ruhr and Rhineland. This was really a
continuation of the campaign against communications which Bomber Command had been required
to carry out during the Battle of France, when any
damage we did to railways, bridges and the like was
quickly repaired or easily by-passed. But it was
probably not until we ourselves had experience of
bomb damage to railways during the Blitz that it
was fully understood how very quickly all but the
heaviest and most widespread and continuous damage can be repaired.

Harris was an extremely clear thinker and he soon
realised that there were only three alternatives when
Britain stood alone against Germany in 1940–41. The
first was to give in, which, as he said, was 'unthinkable'.
The second was to accept a stalemate and to dig in
defensively. He felt that that would ultimately lead to a
victory for 'Nazidom'. The third was to take the fight to
Germany, and the only means available was the bombing
offensive. He wrote later:

If we could keep ahead of the Germans [technolog-ically] I was convinced, having watched the burning of London, that a bomber offensive of adequate weight and with *the right type of bombs* would, if continued for long enough, be something that no country in the world could endure.

THE WELLESLEY

The first bomber that Wallis designed was a biplane tor-pedo bomber codenamed M.1/30. Inevitably, he employed some of the techniques he had developed on the R100, notably the use of light duralumin for wing-spars, lon-gerons and fuselage struts. Wallis also used the same method for riveting the longerons as on the R100.

Vickers' superb test pilot, Mutt Summers, flew the M.1/30 for the first time on 11 January 1933 and con-tinued to test it and suggest modifications throughout that year. However, on 23 November 1933 it broke up in the air when diving at speed for the first time. Summers and his observer, John Radcliffe, escaped by parachute.

Wallis tried to convince the Air Ministry that his next aircraft should be a monoplane. However, the Ministry still favoured biplanes, and Wallis was forced to concur. Nevertheless, he managed to persuade Vickers that he should also design a monoplane and, as a result, two versions of G.4/31 were produced. He was moving towards his geodetic construction concept, but had not fully achieved it. Initially, the Ministry ordered 150 of the biplane version.

The Vickers staff at Weybridge were greatly depressed

by this decision, but at a board meeting on 12 April 1932 the directors decided to build the monoplane at the company's own expense. The biplane first flew on 16 August 1934, and it was after trials at Martlesham that the Air Ministry decided to order the 150. On 19 June 1935 the monoplane made its maiden flight, and it was immediately apparent that its performance was infinitely superior to that of the biplane. Sir Robert McLean wrote to Air Vice-Marshal Sir Hugh Dowding on 5 July 1935:

> I suggest to you that it might be better to reduce these orders in numbers [for the biplane] and in their place go into production of the monoplane as soon as tooling up can be completed. Meantime, and until you can decide whether we shall be allowed to switch over from the biplane to the monoplane, I do not wish to proceed with work on the biplane because, in my view, it is not a modern machine.

His plea was effective, and on 10 September 1935 Vickers was instructed to drop the biplane programme and proceed with the construction of 79 monoplanes. By this time the monoplane had been named the Wellesley. It was single-engined – the engine chosen was the Bristol Pegasus XX – and was a low-wing monoplane with a retractable undercarriage and a top speed of 220 mph at 17,000 feet. Although conceived as a general-purpose aircraft, it was used as a bomber. Above all, it was a long-range aircraft and, at the end of 1937, five Wellesleys were sent from the Vickers production line to the Long-Range Development Unit of the Air Force. On 5 November 1938, three of these Wellesleys left Ismailia bound for

Australia. Two of them landed in Darwin on 7 November, having covered a distance of 7,159 miles. This was a remarkable achievement, but not universally popular. A senior Air Staff officer remarked: 'It will encourage that fellow Wallis to go on with geodetic construction.' Some of the Air Staff remained suspicious of such construction.

An order for another seventeen Wellesleys soon followed, and in the middle of 1936, a third order for another 80. This gave Wallis the opportunity to develop his geodetic construction to the full. He wrote: 'The Wellesley is metal constructed on an entirely new principle – The Vickers-Wallis "Geodetic" system.'

In a paper entitled 'Vickers Wellesley Long-Range Medium Bomber (Pegasus engine) – Vickers-Wallis Geodetic Construction', he wrote:

All parts of the structure are formed as geodetics in the streamline shape of the fuselage, and also in the curved profile of the wings … This method of aeroplane construction is the most important contribution to aircraft engineering since the completion of the first successful metal aircraft. For example, it permits each wing to be hollow and entirely free from any kind of obstruction – the additional space thus gained can be utilised for extra tankage or other loads, and the complete structure is one of extreme lightness combined with great strength and rigidity, thus making possible a range and load carrying capacity that has hitherto been considered unattainable.

Harald Penrose wrote in his *British Aviation 1935–39, The Ominous Skies*:

> Undoubtedly the speed superiority of the 200 mph prototype was a telling factor in securing the order although the rate of climb was somewhat slower than other competitors; but it was also a personal triumph for Barnes Wallis, whom the Air Ministry rated highly for the ingenuity with which his R100 design philosophy was translated into the geodetics of the Wellesley. Nevertheless its production facility and operational robustness had still to be proved, and that Vickers would embark on so daring an innovation emphasised the isolation of Mitchell and his Supermarine team from that of the Pierson-Wallis outlook – for with the Schneider monoplanes and metal-hulled flying-boats a proved technique of metal skimming was already available and could have been successfully adopted by Vickers at less cost than the geodetic system.

THE WELLINGTON

However, such was the pace of development that the Wellesley was obsolete almost before it flew, though it did see active service in the early part of the Second World War, both in support of Wavell in North Africa and in Slim's battle for Keren.

It was quickly followed, and effectively replaced, by the Wellington. It was fortunate that the Wellington, a heavy bomber, was under development, for the light and medium bombers being built at the same time were to prove singularly ineffective in wartime. Three thousand Fairey Battles were produced, and were to suffer heavy losses in France in 1940. Of the 5,400 Bristol Blenheims built, many never saw action, as they were too slow for daytime use. They enjoyed, if that is the right word, a spell as night-fighters and night-bombers, but were withdrawn in the summer of 1942.

As early as October 1932, Vickers received from the Air Ministry a request for a specification of a twin-engined medium day-bomber which possessed a good performance 'envelope' and was capable of carrying a 'useful' load over a good distance at a reasonable speed. This seemed a bit vague; more specifically, the Air Ministry asked for a minimum range of 720 miles carrying a 1,000-lb bomb load. It also specified that the empty, all-up weight should not exceed 6,300 lb. Vickers' tender in February 1933 for B.9/32 was for a full geodetic construction aircraft, and this was effectively the forerunner of the Wellington.

The Wellington was the result of close co-operation on design by Wallis and Pierson, who were soon pushing at the limits laid down in the specification. If Wallis and Pierson had stuck to this, they would not have been able to install the most powerful engine available and the structural weight would have been limited, thus giving a slower aircraft with reduced carrying capacity. They persuaded Vickers and the Ministry that a tare weight of 11,500 lb was possible.

On 15 June 1936, the Wellington took off on its first flight, piloted by Summers and with Wallis and the general manager at Weybridge, Trevor Westbrook, on board.

Its performance showed a great improvement over its specification. Its maximum range was almost double the 1,500 miles prescribed (the 720 miles had been increased to 1,500), and under normal conditions it could carry twice the number of bombs specified.

C.F. Andrews, in his book *Vickers Aircraft Since 1908*, points out that:

> The fuel capacity was raised to 696 gallons, the bomb-load set at 4,300 lb and the all-up weight for production models estimated at 21,000 lb. It was realised that the geodetic construction of the wing promised a bonus that in earlier designs had not been possible. Outboard of the engine nacelles between the front and rear spars there was an unimpeded space and it was decided to use this space in each wing for three separate fuel tanks, all of them capable of being isolated in the event of fire.

The prototype that Summers flew, codenamed K4049, did not last long. On 19 April 1937, during its final trials out of Martlesham, it could not cope with a high-speed dive and broke up, forcing its pilot to escape by parachute (his flight observer was not so lucky, and died in the subsequent crash).

By this time, and in spite of the crash of the prototype Wellington, the Air Ministry had accepted Wallis's geodetic construction. The geodetic bomber and other developments had so transformed the prospects of the Air Force that the Air Ministry was able to propose a much more effective programme of aircraft to be in place by the end of 1939.

Because geodetic construction was completely unknown to most manufacturers, Vickers faced the problem of convincing suppliers – and indeed those in the 'shadow factories' used to manufacture the Wellington – that it was a relatively simple form of construction. It was a great help that the Vickers production team at the main Weybridge plant, led by Trevor Westbrook, devised all the vital tools, jigs and production procedures.

Production of Wellingtons was shared out between the factory at Weybridge and the two shadow factories, at Hawarden near Chester and at Blackpool. That Westbrook and his team did a first-class job is shown by the fact that 9,000 of the 11,460 Wellingtons produced were manufactured at the two shadow factories.

In the early part of the war, before the Wellington got fully into its stride as a bomber, it was used a great deal on 'leaflet raids'. However, even on these, enough experience was gained to show the advantages of Wallis's geodetic system. *The Aeroplane* wrote:

> Wellingtons have returned from raids so damaged that they would appear to be about to collapse at any moment. Yet the geodetic structure spreads the loads so well that even though large portions might be shot away the machines have been able to return to their bases ... The distribution of loads and the high degree of redundancy in the structure make the geodetic system of great military value in keeping losses to a minimum.

Although the Wellington was designed as a bomber, it quickly adapted itself to other roles – submarine hunter-killer, torpedo-strike anti-shipping weapon, reconnaissance eye, supply and freight workhorse, mercy ambulance, VIP and troop transporter, communications hack and experimental vehicle and test-bed.

One of the big threats to Britain in the early part of the war was German attacks on shipping, not only by submarines but also by magnetic mines. From November 1939 to April 1940, losses from mines exceeded those from submarine attacks. The Admiralty, desperately short of minesweepers, asked Vickers whether it was possible to develop a mine-destroying apparatus that could be operated from aircraft. Vickers asked Wallis to work on the project, and the Wellington was chosen for the task. Three Wellington IAs were stripped of all unnecessary fittings and equipped with coils carrying 310 amps at 110 volts DC. These 'degaussing' coils caused the magnetic mines to explode when the aircraft was flown over them at low altitude.

Unfortunately the coils produced a strong magnetic field, rendering the aircraft's compass useless and making navigation impossible. The solution that Wallis suggested was to provide a pilot Wellington sufficiently far ahead as to be out of range of the detonating coil. By December 1939 the problem seemed to have been solved anyway, as Admiralty experts discovered that if the aircraft's compass was adjusted *after* the aircraft had been subjected to the full strength of the coil's magnetic field, then compass readings were sufficiently reliable for the pilot to reach home, even in fog.

The first test flight took place in December 1939, with Mutt Summers as pilot and Wallis as crew. This was deemed successful, and by January 1940 six Wellingtons were carrying out minesweeping operations. Flying just 40 feet above the water, they were responsible for an eighth of all mines detonated by May 1940. However, Wellingtons were needed for other vital work, and these mine-clearing operations were discontinued – although they were revived later in the more confined waters of the Mediterranean and the Suez Canal.

The first production Wellington I (L4212) made its initial flight on 23 December 1937. This aircraft was fitted with Pegasus X engines, but all subsequent Wellington Is had Pegasus XVIIIs. The production Wellington differed considerably from the prototype. The fuselage was re-designed and the characteristic tail fin and rudder supplanted the Stranraer tail (a smaller tail taken from the Stranraer flying boat). The tailwheel was made retractable and gun turrets were fitted; Vickers nose and tail turrets were supplemented by a Nash and Thompson ventral turret. In the Wellington IA (183 built), the Vickers turrets were replaced by Nash and Thompson turrets in the nose and tail, and with the Mark IC (2,685 built), the most common variant in the early days of the war, the ventral gun was replaced by beam guns, the electrical system was modified, and the main wheels were increased in size so that they projected from the engine nacelle when retracted.

The Wellington, known affectionately to both the RAF and the public as the 'Wimpy', was so called after a character named J. Wellington Wimpy, a stout American who enjoyed his hamburgers and who featured in the 'Popeye' strip cartoon in *The Daily Mirror*. The aero-plane was originally going to be called the Crecy, but on 8 September 1936, at Vickers' request, the name was changed to the Wellington. This name, as with the Wellesley, had an obvious connection with the Duke of Wellington, the Iron Duke. The use of 'W' names for the geodetic-constructed Vickers aircraft would continue with the Warwick and the Windsor. It was also a compliment, whether deliberate or not, to Barnes Wallis.

The first Wellington was delivered to 99 Squadron RAF on 10 October 1938, ahead of schedule and shortly after Prime Minister Neville Chamberlain had returned from his meeting with Adolf Hitler promising 'peace for our time'.

The most successful aircraft of the war were those capable of extensive and continual modification: the Spitfire, Hurricane, Mosquito, Lancaster and Wellington. The Wellington appeared in many versions and with several different engines. The Bristol Pegasus engine was soon replaced by the Rolls-Royce Merlin, although the Bristol Hercules and even the Pratt and Whitney Twin Wasp were used. The Wellington also had a number of different roles. The Mark VI, for instance, was used as a high-altitude bomber with a ceiling of 38,500 feet, more than twice the ceiling of the Mark I. By 1940, the Vickers factory at Weybridge had systematised the advantages of the Wellington's geodetic structure by working out methods of repairs according to which geodetic members could be either patched or cut out and replaced.

The Wellington could fairly claim to be the backbone of Bomber Command's night raids over Germany for a long period in the opening phases of the war, before four-engined bombers took over the task in large numbers. At one time in the winter of 1941–42 there were no fewer than 21 squadrons of Wellingtons operational with

Bomber Command, and in the first 1,000-bomber raids on Cologne in May 1942, over half the aircraft taking part were Wellingtons. Chiefly by virtue of its ingenious geodetic lattice-work construction, the Wellington was immensely strong and could take any amount of punishment from flak and return safely home again.

They delivered heavy attacks on all the main targets in Germany, and also raided Italy. On the night of 25–26 August 1940, nine Wellingtons of 99 Squadron and eight of 149 Squadron joined twelve Hampdens and fourteen Whitleys in the first Bomber Command attack on Berlin. On the night of 30 May 1942, no fewer than 599 Wellingtons took part in the historic raid on Cologne. On 1 April 1941, a Wellington of 149 Squadron dropped the first 4,000-lb 'block-buster' bomb during a raid on Emden, and on 15 August 1942, Wellingtons of 109 and 156 Squadrons joined the newly-formed Pathfinder Force. On 5 August 1941, Sergeant J.A. Ward (RNZAF) became the first and only member of a Wellington crew to be awarded the VC. This was for his gallantry when flying as second pilot in an aircraft of 75 Squadron during a night raid on 7 July 1941.

In September 1940, Wellingtons of 37, 38 and 70 Squadrons became the first long-range bombers in the Middle East, where they formed 202 Group. 70 Squadron made the first night attack on Benghazi on 19 September. They did invaluable work in the North African campaigns, and also served in Greece. By the time of El Alamein in November 1942, six Wellington squadrons were in action. Wellingtons were also the first RAF long-range bombers in the Far East, where they operated with 99 and 215 Squadrons in India from the beginning of 1942.

By the autumn of 1943, Wellingtons had completed their useful life with Bomber Command, and the last operational flight was made on the night of 8–9 October. The total tonnage of bombs dropped from home bases was 42,440. Total production of Wellingtons was 11,461, including 3,406 built at Squires Gate, Blackpool, where the last one was delivered on 13 October 1945. By September 1943, when the last Wellington, a Mark XIV, left the Weybridge factory, no fewer than 2,515 had been built there.

THE LANCASTER

The Lancaster bomber is highly relevant to the Barnes Wallis story because, as we shall see, it was a group of modified Lancasters that carried out the raid on the Ruhr dams.

As rearmament pressures built up during the 1930s, specifications for bombers progressed from medium bombers carrying relatively light loads to heavy aircraft capable of higher speeds and the carrying of larger bomb loads.

Specification B.12/36, issued in July 1936, addressed the bomb-load capability and P.13/36, issued in September 1936, concentrated on aircraft performance. P.13/36, described as a heavy bomber, would have a crew of six, two Rolls-Royce Vulture engines and a bomb load capacity of 8,000 lb. A further requirement was that it should be capable of carrying two 21-inch torpedoes for anti-shipping activity. This was significant, in that it meant that the aircraft would have a large bomb compartment, enabling it to carry bigger bombs later on in the war.

The two designs chosen to compete for P.13/36 came from Handley Page and A.V. Roe. The Handley Page aircraft became the Halifax, a moderately successful bomber of which 6,176 were built. A.V. Roe's proposal was for an aircraft 69 feet in length, with a 72-foot wingspan, a gross weight of 37,000 lb, a top speed of 330 mph at 15,000 feet and a service ceiling of 24,000 feet. Designated the Manchester, two prototypes were ordered on 8 September 1936. In charge of design was Avro's Chief Designer, Roy Chadwick, who had already enjoyed success with the Avro 500 series. (Indeed, the Avro 504 had carried out the first bombing raid on Germany in the First World War.)

Development of the Manchester was relatively slow, but by late 1940 most problems seemed to have been ironed out and expectations were high that it could carry the fight to the heartland of Germany, a task beyond the reach of the existing medium bombers. However, there were still problems with the Vulture engines, which lacked the necessary power and were prone to overheating.

In his book *The Avro Lancaster*, Francis Mason goes into great detail about the development of the Manchester and its replacement by the Lancaster. His conclusion is that pressure for a new bomber forced the pace too hard, for both the airframe and the engine manufacturer. The origin of the Rolls-Royce Vulture was the search for a high-powered engine with more potential than the Buzzard. The Rolls-Royce Buzzard was a scaled-up Kestrel, itself a scale-up from Sir Henry Royce's first aero engine, the Eagle, which he had developed in 1914. The first prototype of the Vulture ran in September 1937, the second in January 1938 and the third in May 1938.

Following lessons learnt, a prototype Vulture II, with a two-speed supercharger, ran in September 1938.

Testing continued in 1939 and, in the light of experience with the Merlin and other engines, major modifications were made to Vulture I so that Vulture II appeared not only with an improved supercharger, but also with a down-draught carburettor, a modified ignition set-up, and a number of other improvements. It passed its type-test quite quickly and went into production. However, it soon ran into problems.

The first was that one half of the split cooling system could airlock and the coolant flow into two cylinder blocks could cease, with subsequent piston seizure. Once the mechanism was established, the cure, a balancing bleed between the two coolant pumps, was not difficult. The second problem was more serious and more difficult: bearing and con-rods which had a gudgeon pin at each end, one in the piston and the other in a similar bearing in the master rod big-end. Originally it was thought that the problem lay in the master rod big-end, but deeper investigations indicated that the two halves of the crankcase had been moving relative to each other. The problem was cured by fitting one-inch-diameter steel dowels in each crankcase end panel to ensure positive location of the two halves with each other.

The Vulture V with these various modifications was a very satisfactory engine, even at ratings higher than the Vulture II. There were some continuing difficulties, but these were allied to the installation rather than the engine. The Manchester suffered from design faults on the airframe, and it was soon realised that the wingspan would need to be increased and extra tail fins added. The

Vulture engine was prone to two sorts of failure. First, it tended to throw con-rods, either through lack of oil or because of the mechanical loads on the big-ends at maximum rpm. Second, it overheated and the Glycol coolant caught fire. This was not the fault of the Vulture engine itself, but rather of the installation, designed by Avro. The cowling was too close to the engine, and did not allow sufficient ventilation.

However, the damage had been done. The Manchester had already built up a bad reputation from which it would be difficult to recover, and Avro were now looking into the four Merlin engine idea. The Merlin had proved itself in the Spitfire and Hurricane, and Ernest Hives, the General Manager of Rolls-Royce, had become convinced that the Manchester should be powered by four reliable Merlins rather than two, as yet unproven, Vultures.

The Manchester began operations early in 1941 but suffered heavy losses in the first half of the year, many of them caused by engine failure. By the end of that year there were still only four squadrons of Manchesters in operation, and during 1942 this was reduced to three. Nevertheless, 46 Manchesters participated in the first 1,000-bomber raid on Cologne on the night of 30–31 May 1942. That night also saw a feat of bravery for one of the Manchester pilots, Flying Officer Leslie Manser, who refused to bail out but kept his aircraft steady on one engine while the rest of his crew did so. He did not escape. For this he was awarded the Victoria Cross. Manchesters also took part in the second and third 1,000-bomber raids on Essen and Bremen, but by the middle of 1942 the operational life of this aircraft was effectively over.

The life of the Lancaster, as the Manchester Mark III

was called, was about to begin. Even before the war, Chadwick had begun work on the Manchester airframe to adapt it to be able to take four engines instead of two.

Ronnie Harker, one of Rolls-Royce's liaison test pilots, remembered that although the Vulture problems were overcome, it was not before a number of Manchesters were lost, and he witnessed the loss of the test aircraft. It should be noted that a number of the crashes were not caused by the failure of the Vulture engine.

Harker wrote later in his book, *The Engines Were Rolls-Royce*:

I happened to have flown over to Ternhill Aerodrome where I was giving a talk to the pilots of the fighter conversion unit. I was standing on the aerodrome talking to Squadron Leader Gerry Edge who, incidentally, was to become godfather to my second daughter! He was a good friend of mine and I had joined his 605 Squadron at the end of the Battle of Britain, where it was operating from Croydon. It had been the first squadron equipped with the Hurricane Mark II. Group Captain Teddy Donaldson, who was the station commander, was also with us.

We saw a Manchester approaching the aerodrome with one engine on fire. The pilot, Reg Curlew, one of our test pilots, and very experienced on large multi-engined aircraft, seemed to be well in control; he was making a downwind approach with enough height, so it seemed, to be able at least to turn and land across-wind. He must have thought he could get round into wind, so he continued the

1. Airship R26, built by Vickers. Its first trial flight was in autumn 1917. The R26 was part of the R23 class, which H.B. Pratt and Barnes Wallis developed for Vickers when they rejoined the company in November 1915 following a short spell in the forces.

2. The famous R100 airship, developed and built by the Airship Guarantee Company at Howden in Yorkshire during the second half of the 1920s. Barnes Wallis acted as Chief Engineer, with Nevil Shute-Norway (later better known as the author Nevil Shute) as his assistant. It made its first long-haul flight to Canada and back in the summer of 1930. Following the crash of its rival, the R101, the R100 never flew again.

3. The R101 airship. Developed and built at the same time as the privately-financed R100, the government-backed R101 prepared for its first long-haul flight – to India – just after the R100 returned from Canada. Unfortunately, it crashed at Beauvais in France, killing all but six of the 54 people on board. It was the end of airship development in Britain.

4. Geodetic construction. Following the collapse of hopes for the airship, Wallis concentrated his efforts on heavier-than-air aircraft, and developed a new type of construction, geodetic construction, described as follows: 'Geodetics are the shortest distance between two points on any curved surface – derived from the "great-circle" principle of mathematics utilised in trans-ocean navigation.'

5 and 6. Two monoplanes built using Wallis's geodetic construction. When Wallis began work on bombers for Vickers in the early 1930s, the Air Ministry still favoured biplanes. Wallis persuaded Vickers that the future was monoplanes, and they concurred enough to allow him to develop both. Initially the Ministry ordered 150 biplanes, but when the Vickers-financed monoplane was tested, it became abundantly clear that its performance was infinitely superior to the biplane. The biplane was dropped and Wallis's geodetic monoplane replaced it.

7. The Wellesley bomber showing Wallis's geodetic construction. Wallis wrote: 'All parts of the structure are formed as geodetics in the streamline shape of the fuselage, and also in the curved profile of the wings ... This method of aeroplane construction is the most important contribution to aircraft engineering since the completion of the first successful metal aircraft.'

8. The Wellesley was a single-engined – the engine chosen was the Bristol Pegasus XX – low-winged bomber with a top speed of 220 mph at 17,000 feet.

9. On 5 November 1938, two long-range Wellesleys made a record-breaking long-distance flight to Australia. They flew non-stop for two days from Egypt to Darwin, Australia, a distance of 7,162 miles. Unsuited to the European air war, the Wellesley was nevertheless used effectively in East Africa, Egypt and the Middle East from 1940 to 1942.

circuit before turning into wind for the final approach. Alas, he undershot and landed just short of the aerodrome in a field which had some large trees in it. He hit one of these and a wing was pulled off, rupturing the fuel tank; there was an explosion and the whole aeroplane went up in flames. We rushed to the spot in the group captain's car only to find a mass of flames; the two flight observers had managed to crawl out of the rear door and were not badly burned but there was no sign of Reg Curlew. Gerry Edge and Teddy Donaldson, amidst the exploding ammunition, did get into the aircraft by the rear door for a few moments. Gerry Edge said he saw the pilot still in his seat but crushed against the control column and obviously either dead or unconscious. One of the tyres then burst, the aircraft settled down and another tank burst so Gerry made a hurried retreat, getting out just in the nick of time before the whole thing became one mass of flames.

Major George Bulman, a key figure at the Air Ministry, recalled after this crash:

Air Marshal Tedder and Sir Wilfrid Freeman went to Avros just after this prototype had spun in, and Dobbie Dobson the irrepressible [Sir Roy Dobson, managing director of A.V. Roe Ltd], with a model Manchester in his hand, said none of them were happy with the results to date and that Rolls-Royce seemed lukewarm about the Vultures. Whereupon he slipped off the model's wing and replaced it with another mounting four Merlins. Hence the

Lancaster which was destined to become the best British bomber of the war.

It gradually became clear that this aircraft was going to be greatly superior to the original Manchester, and the orders given for Manchesters were modified so that Lancasters replaced them. The Lancasters began operations during the winter of 1941–42 and immediately proved both popular and successful. Build-up during 1942 was slow, but by the end of that year twelve operational squadrons were using about 200 aircraft. There were fears that the Rolls-Royce Merlin engine, either manufactured in Britain or brought over from Packard in the USA, would not be able to keep pace because of demand for the engine for other aircraft, but these fears proved groundless. By mid-1943, 23 squadrons had been equipped with Lancasters. As we shall see, Lancasters were to play a vital part in Wallis's Second World War career.

This was 'Bomber' Harris's verdict on it:

The finest bomber of the war! Its efficiency was almost incredible, both in performance and in the way it could be saddled with ever-increasing loads without breaking the camel's back. The Lancaster far surpassed all the other types of heavy bombers. Not only could it take heavier bomb loads, not only was it easier to handle, and not only were there fewer accidents than with other types, the casualty rate was also consistently below those of other types.

The Lancaster took the major part in winning the war with its attacks on Germany. On land it forced the Germans to retrieve from their armies half their sorely needed anti-tank guns for use by over a million soldiers who would otherwise have been serving in the field. The Lancaster won the naval war by destroying over one third of the German submarines in their ports, together with hundreds of small naval craft and six of their largest warships. Above all, the Lancaster won the air war by taking the major part in forcing Germany to concentrate on building and using fighters to defend the Fatherland, thereby depriving their armies of essential air and particularly bomber support.

CHAPTER THREE

WAR AGAIN

METHOD OF ATTACK

After the Wellesley and the Wellington, Wallis turned his thoughts to the development of larger bombs and therefore larger bombers. He was supported by Pierson, who had proposed that Vickers produce a six-engine geodetic bomber with a wingspan of 235 feet and a 20-ton bomb load, which would have the equivalent destructive power of a whole squadron of Wellingtons.

Wallis found his supervision of the Wellington's development insufficient to satisfy his craving to make a more significant contribution to the war effort, and he worked at home on his ideas for big bombs and big bombers. He wrote to his old friend, Commander Masterman:

> Life is almost unrelieved gloom – worse than 25 years ago, except that this time I can feel that I am doing something useful whereas last war I certainly was not – in spite of your efforts to convince me to the contrary ... Tremendously busy – on big developments, which if they had been put in hand two years ago would have won us the war by this time.
>
> Too late as usual.

Wallis was no expert on bombs – his experience was in aircraft design – but he set himself the task of learning everything he could about them. He said later:

Autumn 1939 to Autumn 1940 I spent learning about bombs, the behaviour, chemistry and elementary physics of High Explosives; the construction of the Winding Shafts of German collieries; the Construction of Gravity, Multiple Arch and Earth Dams.

Wallis probed at both the Air Ministry and the Ministry of Aircraft Production for information on dams, especially the Möhne, and gathered some useful information from an F.W.R. Leistikow who worked for a patent agency in Chancery Lane. He produced articles from the *Zeitschrift für Bauwesen* in 1919 and the *Zeitschrift für Die Gesamte Wasserwirtschaft* of April 1906.

With coal mines, Wallis foresaw that it would be virtually impossible to collapse the galleries and tunnels hundreds of feet underground. The winding-shaft would be vulnerable but would be easily repaired. As for oil wells and dumps, the Romanian oil-fields were too far away, and the refineries and dumps too heavily defended.

In preparation for presentation of his ideas, he built a profile of the German economy, including the distribution of oil storage tanks and dams. He also continued to study the behaviour, chemistry and physics of high explosives and the propagation of waves in all types of soil. He proved the theory that bombers could operate at 40,000 feet.

A meeting with the Minister for Aircraft Production,

Lord Beaverbrook, was organised in the summer of 1940 and Wallis convinced him that the British already possessed in the Wellington a bomber capable of flying at 40,000 feet. Beaverbrook thought that it was only the Americans who had one.

Once he knew that he had Beaverbrook's support, he bombarded everyone he could think of with the idea. However, there was a great deal of opposition, much of it sensibly based on the fact that, at the time, there was no stabilised bomb-sight. A bomber carrying a single bomb, however big and destructive it might be, was a sortie wasted if the bomb, as was most likely, missed its target.

Nevertheless, Beaverbrook wrote to Vickers on 9 January 1941:

High-altitude bombers are to be developed intensively; I wish you to undertake this work.

The Wellington V is to be fully developed with Hercules and Merlin engines. The Merlin to take preference. The B1/35 is to have a pressure cabin; the work is to be pursued urgently.

The Centaurus engine [manufactured by the Bristol Engine Company] will be developed for use with this aircraft.

This must have seemed encouraging to Wallis, but Beaverbrook concluded:

Subject to the above work [development of the Wellington] taking precedence, you should continue research on your 50-ton bomber.

Thus half-encouraged, Wallis produced a document which showed not only where all the key production elements of Germany were, but how they could best be put out of action by large penetration bombs. These were the opening paragraphs of Wallis's seminal work, 'A Note on a Method of Attacking the Axis Powers':

1. The Bomb Armament of all the belligerent Air Forces in this War consists of relatively small bombs designed to attack surface targets such as factories and houses.

2. This form of attack is effectively countered by dispersal. It is becoming impossible to destroy simultaneously <u>all</u> the factories and <u>all</u> the generating stations all over the continent of Europe.

3. All these factories are however dependent upon relatively few and highly localised Stores of Energy in the form of Coal, Oil and Water Power; air attacks on this country are dependent upon large stores of petrol buried in tanks many feet underground.

4. The Stores of Energy are so concentrated and so massive that they cannot be dispersed, but also they are <u>invulnerable</u> to the present type of Bomb Armament.

5. This paper shows that:
1) These stores of energy are vulnerable to very large bombs.
2) By sterilising their Stores of Energy the industries of Germany and Italy can be quickly paralysed.

3) The very large bomb and appropriate bomb-carrying aircraft are practicable and can be produced in this country.

He was greatly helped in compiling his data by officials in Whitehall, but most notably by Wing Commander F.W. Winterbotham. Morpurgo describes Winterbotham as follows:

A one-time Oxford law student, one-time Yeomanry officer, one-time Royal Flying Corps pilot and one-time farmer, he had returned to the RAF to a desk job that served as cover for high-grade intelligence operations which had taken him into the presence and close to the confidence of many among the Nazi leadership. Winterbotham it was who, with his French opposite number, originated early in the 'thirties' the technique and practice of high-altitude spying.

Winterbotham and Wallis became close friends and Winterbotham succeeded in getting Wallis's ideas into the Cabinet Office. The reply was not encouraging:

I have not only read your interesting paper on the ultimate aim of bombing warfare, but have consulted certain good-willed experts without disclosing your identity.

The view held is that such a project as you describe could not come to fruition until 1942, if then. This may not be a complete bar since the war may still be going on in that year.

It is suggested, however, that if the plan is to be put into effect in a reasonable period the best thing to do is to take it up with the Boeing Company or some other American firm used to work of this type.

Winterbotham was as good an ally and supporter as Wallis could have hoped for, but even he found Wallis's impatience and intolerance of others a little trying at times. When Winterbotham had received a somewhat negative reply from Major Desmond Morton in the Prime Minister's office on 5 July 1940 and conveyed it to Wallis, he noted Wallis's annoyance and wrote:

In those very early days Barnes could not envisage the possibility of anybody not falling in with his ideas at once.

Undeterred, Wallis sent out over 100 copies of 'Method of Attack', four of them to people in the still neutral United States.

Finally, in March 1941, the Chief of the Air Staff, Sir Henry Tizard, set up an ad hoc committee to look into Wallis's proposals and showed, by the calibre of those on the committee, how seriously he took them.

The chairman was Dr David Pye, Director of Scientific Research at the Air Ministry, and no fewer than four members were, or soon would be, Fellows of the Royal Society. The Committee met for the first time on Good Friday, 11 April 1941, and the minutes stated that 'those present agreed to recommend that some means of attacking German and Italian Power Installations be considered'. The power installations most favoured for attack were dams, and a special Dams Committee was formed.

With the help of Dr Glanville of the Road Research Laboratory, Wallis made a series of models of the largest dams. Wallis's favoured target was the Möhne, perhaps because when it had been built by the Kaiser in 1913, the Germans had been so proud of it that they had given out detailed technical information about it. Wallis built an exact scale reproduction at Harmondsworth and months of experiment followed, only to provide a depressing conclusion.

To achieve the result, Wallis thought it necessary for the bomb to carry a charge-weight of 30,000 lb and this, when cased, would give a bomb-weight of 60,000 lb. This was beyond the carrying capacity of any existing bomber.

Disappointed but undeterred, Wallis set his mind to devising a different type of bomb. He thought the answer might lie in a spherical bomb. He had studied the propensities of spheres (and had even suggested a cricket ball which batsmen would find unplayable!), and knew that they possessed good ballistic properties and would have a more accurate flight path than an ordinary bomb. He thought that they would be good for underwater bombing where rapid deceleration and good water-stability were required.

MYTHS ABOUT THE DAMS RAID

The main sources of information about the raids by 617 Squadron on the dams in the Ruhr on 17 May 1943 were, for a long time, Guy Gibson's book *Enemy Coast Ahead*, written during the war before his tragic death in 1944, and Paul Brickhill's *The Dambusters*, published in 1949. These were followed by a very successful and popular film, *The Dam Busters*, starring Michael Redgrave as Barnes Wallis.

In 1982, a book called *The Dams Raid: Epic or Myth*, by Dr John Sweetman, dispelled many of the myths that had grown up about the raid. In the Preface to his very heavily researched book, Sweetman wrote:

> For security reasons, the story that emerged ... was necessarily incomplete and even, in some respects, deliberately misleading. With official records also closed to the public for another thirty years, further inaccuracies and embellishments gradually became an integral part of the legend.

Sweetman pointed out that Gibson's book did not give details of the full operational plan or the bombs used. The 1955 film was even more misleading, and the producer admitted to Barnes Wallis that simplification had been essential. For example, it showed Gibson watching the spotlights on a line of chorus girls in a theatre and using the idea to establish the correct height for the aircraft attacking the dams. In reality Benjamin Lockspeiser, a civilian scientist, suggested an idea that had been used for the hunting of submarines. Most of all, the film portrayed the single-mindedness of Wallis eventually overcoming the reluctance of officials. Sweetman wrote:

> The film also popularised the claim that Barnes Wallis developed single-handed the special weapon

used against the dams, in the face of reluctant (in his view 'singularly stupid') senior officers and obstructive civil servants. Undoubtedly, he did have an uphill struggle to convince responsible authorities that he had the means to breach the dams. But the Air Staff had long recognised their importance (especially the Möhne and Sorpe). Since 1937, it had vainly been seeking a way of destroying them; and these efforts intensified once war broke out ... And it is clear that, certainly from mid-1940 onwards, Wallis did have access to official files and received considerable assistance from civilian and Service authorities.

Sweetman did not want to belittle Wallis's achievement, but he wanted others to be credited for their contributions. His Preface continued:

Acknowledging that Wallis did have valuable official help during his three-year quest for the wherewithal to destroy the German dams, and access to previous schemes for doing so, should not in any sense detract from his unique achievement in designing the ultimate weapon and refining the technique for its delivery. None the less, it is a fact that a wide range of organisations throughout ... Britain did contribute expertise, advice and invaluable effort to the project: the Road Research Laboratory; Building Research Station; National Physical Laboratory; Royal Ordnance Factories at Chorley and Woolwich; Vickers Armstrong facilities at Newcastle, Barrow, Weybridge, Burhill and Crayford; A.V.

Roe and Co. Ltd at Manchester; the Royal Aircraft Establishment at Farnborough; the Armament and Aeronautical Experimental Establishment at Boscombe Down; and smaller manufacturing concerns like the Oxley Engineering Company at Leeds and the Limmer and Trinidad Lake Asphalt Company in London, among others.

With regard to the film *The Dam Busters* and Wallis's portrayal by Michael Redgrave, L.R. Day of the National Science Museum wrote:

> I asked Sir Barnes whether he thought the portrayal (in the film, *The Dam Busters*) true to life and he seemed well satisfied with it. Perhaps though, the film character was smoother, less forthright, even less downright awkward than the man himself could be.

PROPELLED PIERCING BOMB

For the sake of simplicity, it is best to concentrate on Wallis's thinking and efforts in developing both the bomb and method of attack on the Ruhr dams and then on his thinking in promoting and developing 'big' bombs, with which he hoped Bomber Command would be able to shorten the war. First, we have to realise what bombs were available, as well as the aircraft to carry them, and consequently how the authorities were thinking.

When war broke out in September 1939, the RAF's existing stock of bombs was extremely old, mainly going back to 1918–19. Efforts to produce more up-to-date and somewhat better bombs had been lackadaisical, and even these new ones were filled with a poor explosive material called amatol. Moreover, only 25 per cent of the weight of the bombs consisted of explosive. There was an attempt in 1926 to develop 1,000-lb bombs, but the Air Staff felt that they would never need a bomb larger than 500 lb, and the attempt stalled. Bombers were designed to carry 500-lb bombs, so 1,000 lb would need bigger, and therefore more expensive, aircraft. The RAF's thinking was: drop more, smaller bombs because they have a better chance of hitting the target than fewer, bigger ones.

The trouble with this thinking, as Barnes Wallis realised, was that the bombs would not do much damage. The problem also was that Germany's factories were widely dispersed. However, the sources of power for those factories – coal mines, oil wells and dumps, and what was known as 'white coal', i.e. dams supplying both water and hydro-electric power – were too big to disperse and hide. Damage them and the source of power would be removed. However, they would not be damaged by small bombs. What was needed was big bombs and therefore, inevitably, big bombers, but maybe also different *types* of bomb, because even big bombs might not be sufficient to damage seriously such large facilities as coal mines, buried oil dumps and dams.

One of Wallis's early supporters was Air Vice-Marshal A.W. Tedder. Unfortunately, at the beginning of the war he was relatively junior and, in late 1940, he was posted from the Ministry of Aircraft Production at Millbank to the Middle East. Wallis wrote to him:

Greatly distressed … I am sorry to lose the

encouragement and support which you have so
consistently given to me.

However, he went on to say that Tedder's support had
not been in vain, and that the Road Research Labora-
tories were agreeing with him about the effect of shock
waves on underwater structures. He continued in his
letter to Tedder:

[They agree with] my forecast that we can, without
much difficulty, destroy all the Italian dams ... A
second report to hand to-day [28 November 1940]
shows that a ten-ton bomb will probably destroy the
Möhne Dam. ...

If only all concerned had been as ready to accept
our original suggestions as you were, this scheme
would be further forward than it actually is. As a
result of the continued opposition that we have met
it has been necessary to resort to these laborious
and long-winded experiments in order to prove that
what I suggested last July can in reality be done.

When Major General Sir Hugh Trenchard became Chief
of the Air Staff in 1918, he said:

There can be no doubt that we must be prepared for
long-distance aerial operations against any enemy's
main source of supply.

In October 1937 the Air Staff had drawn up a list of
thirteen plans, known as the Western Air (WA) Plans, for
use in case of war. WA5 was 'to attack the German War
Industry including the supply of oil with priority to that

in the Ruhr, Rhineland and Saar'. Forty-five power and coking plants were identified as potential targets, and in addition the Air Targets Sub-Committee identified the Möhne and Sorpe dams. Indeed, this Sub-Committee thought that the two dams might be a more viable alternative than the 45 plants. Nevertheless, the committee remained cautious, saying:

> If the policy to attack the dams is accepted the committee are of the opinion that the development of a propelled piercing bomb of high capacity would be essential to ensure the requisite velocity and flight approximating to the horizontal. Even then its success would be highly problematical.

As various committees batted ideas back and forth about how best to destroy the dams, key people in the Air Ministry, the Ministry of Aircraft Production, the Admiralty and research departments at Farnborough and Woolwich became familiar with arguments about the strategic importance of the Ruhr dams and possible ideas of breaching them.

THE DAMS

Dams were different from mines and underground oil installations. The Ruhr dams were close to England and not so easily defended. Three seemed particularly important in their contribution to the German economy: the Möhne, the Eder and the Sorpe.

The Möhne dammed the Möhne Lake, where the River Heve flowed into the Ruhr – vital for coal, steel and tanks going to and from the Ruhr foundries. It held 134 million tons of water.

In his book *The Dams Raid*, Sweetman showed what the experts felt the effect would be of the breaching of the Möhne:

The paper circulated by [Air Chief Marshal Sir Charles] Portal argued that direct destruction by escaping water from the Möhne would be 'appreciable': low-lying districts of the Ruhr, including Herdecke, Welter, Witten, Mattingen, Linden, Kettwig, Mülheim and Duisburg, would suffer. An average rate of flow of 3,720 cubic metres per second would empty the Möhne reservoir in ten hours. The capacity of this reservoir alone is, therefore, great enough to cause a disaster of the first magnitude 'which would spread to densely populated areas' between the Ruhr and Dortmund-Ems canal. 'Substantial' loss of electricity would occur due to the destruction of 13 hydro electric plants between the Möhne Dam and Mülheim on the Ruhr river, of which the Herdecke station was the most important. Even if complete destruction were not achieved, variation of flow in the Ruhr river due to loss of reservoir control should adversely affect electricity production, and the thermo-electricity generating station would also be affected during the summer months. In addition, a 'most serious effect' would occur for foundries, coal mines, coke ovens, blast furnaces and chemical plants if water supplies were restricted. Navigation on the Ruhr would inevitably be interfered with and, in the narrow valley, damage to railways and bridges could not be avoided. So far as domestic water supplies were concerned, the entire Ruhr area eastwards to Hamm and Ahlen depended on the Möhne reservoir. Priority had inevitably to be given to the domestic user and firefighting needs, which in turn would have an additional adverse effect upon industry.

The Eder dammed the Eder River to create the Eder Lake, holding 212 million tons of water and controlling the level of the Mitteland canal, Germany's second most important waterway. The effects of breaching the Eder dam would not be as severe as on the Möhne. When assessing the possible damage, O.L. Lawrence of the Ministry of Economic Warfare said that the Eder had no connection with the Ruhr, and while agricultural land and possibly the low-lying districts of Kassel would be flooded, the Weser River and Mitteland canal would not be 'critically' affected. The four power stations below the dam would 'probably' be destroyed but this would not be of 'major economic importance'.

On the other hand, destruction of the Sorpe Dam which, with the Möhne, supplied 75 per cent of the Ruhr's water, would 'produce a paralysing effect upon the industrial activity in the Ruhr and would result in a further lowering of morale'.

But still Wallis could not see how to produce and carry a bomb heavy enough to be more than a pin-prick on these massive structures. However, he knew that shock waves in the earth or in a solid structure could magnify the explosive effect – and furthermore, he suddenly realised, *in water* as well.

He went back to his drawing board and calculated that a 10-ton bomb exploding deep in water by a dam wall would punch a hole a hundred feet across. That was all very well, but no aircraft existed that could carry a 10-ton bomb to the Ruhr. Furthermore, he felt that the bomb would need to be dropped from about 45,000 feet. Could the bomb-aimer be accurate enough in view of the wind and so on? He calculated that he could, because with a 10-ton bomb, a direct hit was not necessary. The earth-quake effect would be such that the target would be shaken to destruction.

'I HAD THE IDEA OF A MISSILE'

Wallis was concerned that the Air Attack on Dams Committee were close to withdrawing their support, and by the end of 1941 he too felt

> the growing conviction that my original suggestion was impracticable which led me to seek for other methods of destruction ... Early in 1942 I had the idea of a missile, which if dropped on the water at a considerable distance upstream of the dam would reach the dam in a series of ricochets, and after impact against the crest of the dam would sink in close contact with the upstream face of masonry.

According to Sweetman – and he interviewed him – Wallis could not explain how the concept occurred to him. He did not think it could have come from children skimming pebbles across a pond, since they revolve around a vertical axis whereas Wallis's bomb spun around the horizontal. (This seems to me a technicality which does not affect the *principle* of a missile bouncing across water.) Wallis had also learnt of USAAF bombers skipping bombs across the water in low-level attacks on ships.

He was encouraged by his knowledge that Admiral Nelson had used the ability of spheres to ricochet, i.e. bounce, on water, to extend the range of his guns in his sea battles with the French. Not only did Wallis remember reading this, he also recalled that German mathematicians had turned this practice into a mathematical law. A paper of 1921, 'Exterior Ballistics', established that if the angle of incidence is less than seven degrees, the angle of reflection from the water is always less than the angle of incidence.

Wallis was convinced that he had discovered the answer. If the bomb was dropped some distance from the dam wall, it would bounce along the water, hit the wall and sink until detonated by a hydrostatic pistol which would fire when a certain pressure was reached.

He continued to think about it, and in April 1942 began experiments with his children in the garden of his house at Effingham. As Sweetman explained:

Commandeering a supply of his daughter Elisabeth's marbles, he fired them out of a catapult device to ricochet from the surface of the water in a tub and then, clearing a taut string, land second bounce on a table, where the fall of each missile was marked in chalk by the Wallis children ... Wallis patiently collected valuable data, though he was far from establishing the reliable Law of Ricochet which he sought. The shape of the ultimate projectile (sphere or oblong) also concerned him. He explained to Winterbotham that in a spherical bomb, if detonated from the centre, the explosion would reach all points of the surface at the same moment, thus disarming one major criticism directed at his deep-penetration weapon. Without giving him a reason, Wallis asked about the behaviour of a spherical bomb on impact with a surface. Winterbotham rang an Air Ministry contact, who told him that far from achieving deep penetration 'it would bounce like a football'. Wallis's reaction surprised Winterbotham: 'But my dear boy, splendid! Splendid!'

In the middle of April 1942 Wallis approached an old friend, Professor P.M.S. Blackett, scientific adviser to the Admiralty, largely because he thought his new idea had 'become essentially a weapon for the Fleet Air Arm'. He gave Blackett a paper entitled 'Spherical Bomb–Surface Torpedo'. In the paper, Wallis suggested that an aircraft could carry a large spherical bomb, and that this sphere would not be susceptible to initial disturbance by the under-body turbulence of the carrying aircraft at the moment of release, and thus its flight path should in fact be more accurate than that of an ordinary bomb.

Wallis went on to say that, to ensure success, the attacking aircraft must

attain a high velocity close to the surface ... By approaching the target in a fast glide and flattening out the bomb should be dropped from a height not greater than 260 feet when travelling at a speed of

470 feet per second ... This method of attack, permitting the aircraft to turn away at a distance upstream where short-range defences are unlikely to be situated, offers a promising means of obtaining the necessary proximity without undue risk to the aircraft and crew.

Blackett was impressed, but he did not see that the potential effectiveness of the weapon should be restricted to the Navy, and he talked to Sir Henry Tizard about it. Tizard, equally impressed, went to see Wallis at Burhill on 23 April 1942.

Experiments continued in the water tanks at the National Physical Laboratory at Teddington, especially with regard to the benefits of imparting backspin. Vickers Armstrong produced a paper in August 1942 explaining that:

The enhancing lift force due to the reverse spinning motion applied to the missile has three advantageous effects. a). It increases the distance which the missile will travel after release from the carrier, before striking the water; b). It diminishes the tendency of the missile to plunge downwardly on impact with the water surface; c). It increases the distance which the missile will travel whilst ricocheting. As will be understood, all of these effects contribute to the improvement of the effective range.

By June 1942, Wallis was wondering whether a cylinder might be better than a sphere, and he acknowledged that it would be more practical to manufacture.

Through the summer, senior personnel from both the Admiralty and the Air Ministry saw experiments laid on by Wallis, who recorded that the Admiralty were '*tremendously* impressed'. The Air Ministry officials were not so easily convinced, and aroused the ire of Wallis, never slow to show his impatience. He wrote to Major P.L. Teed, a friend at the Ministry of Aircraft Production, on 21 July 1942:

> ... the profound effect of water impact waves has not yet been realised by the Air Force, but is now appreciated by the Admiralty ... There is no doubt that the Air Staff have been singularly stupid over this point.

'ACTUAL CONTACT WITH THE MASONRY'

During the spring of 1942, A.R. Collins, a scientific officer in the concrete section at the Road Research Laboratory, Harmondsworth, had been unofficially carrying out experiments using charges with direct contact to the target. Such experiments had always been ignored on the grounds that such accuracy of bombing would be impossible. The result was a staggering success and undoubtedly influenced Wallis. Thirty years later, Wallis said to Collins:

> The bouncing bomb was originated solely to meet the requirement so convincingly demonstrated by your experiments that actual contact with the masonry of the dam was essential.

Wallis also wrote, just after the war:

Just before this [April 1942], in view of the discouraging results obtained from the experiments authorised by the AAD Committee, I had approached Dr Pye in confidence, telling him that I had an idea which would probably enable a charge to be placed *in contact with the dam face* and *exploded at any required depth*, asking him if he would guide the Committee before issuing their report to recommend a final series of experiments with the object of determining the smallest possible charge that would breach the dam when detonated in actual contact with the masonry together with the depth below the surface at which it should explode.

Collins himself believed his experiment to be crucial, but acknowledged the contribution of his boss, Dr W.H. Glanville, Director of the Road Research Laboratory, towards completing it. He thought that Glanville's advice represented

a crucial turning point in the experimental work because it gave us the confidence to undertake [a] second test on Nant-y-Gro [a dam in Wales] with a real hope of success. If this test had failed, and the dam had been severely damaged but not breached, the case for an attack would have been seriously weakened.

After a further test at Nant-y-Gro, Collins was able to report in August 1942 that a 50-foot breach could be caused by a charge, in contact with the dam wall, of about 7,500 lb exploded 30 feet below the water level. This was within the carrying capacity of the Lancaster. Furthermore, it would release about 70 per cent of the water within the Möhne. Collins felt that this report was

the crucial report of the Road Research Laboratory tests ... It not only showed that (with Glanville's adjustment to allow for gravity) a model would give a reasonable estimate of the size of the breach but also introduced, for the first time, the concept that the 'scale' of an attack with a contact charge was determined by the depth of the charge and not the size of the dam.

After further tests, Wallis wrote in his diary on 29 September 1942:

I see Lord Cherwell and find him unresponsive ... [he] doubted if the Dams were of any consequence.

Frederick Lindemann, Lord Cherwell, as Winston Churchill's closest scientific adviser, was an important figure. An arrogant, bigoted man, no one liked or trusted him. Perversely, that seemed to endear him to Churchill, who had known him since the First World War. Lindemann had become Professor of Experimental Philosophy at Oxford and, as Morpurgo put it:

Churchill followed Lindemann blindly wherever his science fiction led, and seems to have taken no account of Lindemann's zest for bringing the dubious pleasures of academic feuding into national policy-making. In the spring of 1941 Lindemann did not yet know Wallis, but damned him because of Wallis's friends. He was frenetic in his disagreements with other scientists: he detested Tizard, and Professor Blackett, who was also showing interest in Wallis's schemes.

Finally, on 4 December 1942, Mutt Summers, Vickers' test pilot, took off in a Wellington bomber from Weybridge with Wallis as bomb-aimer and Captain R.C. Handasyde of Vickers in the second pilot's seat, and flew to Chesil Beach near Portland in Dorset. The bomb-bay doors had been removed and a special apparatus for spinning and releasing the two practice bombs on board had been installed. Unfortunately the experiment was unsuccessful, with the two welded spheres bursting on impact.

Wallis ordered that the casing be reinforced, and a second test took place on 15 December. Summers dived the Wellington at full speed and released the two spheres – one smooth, one dimpled – at 60 feet, but both shattered on impact. Wallis rowed around for two hours and recovered one.

Undeterred, Wallis continued the tests. The Admiralty, especially, were still keen and suggested trying a smaller bomb. With increasing levels of success, trials continued through January and into February 1943. By this time, Wallis's weapon had been split into two: 'Highball', a smaller one, to be delivered by the relatively small but fast fighter bomber, the Mosquito, against vessels; and 'Upkeep', a larger one, to be delivered by the heavy bomber, the Lancaster, against dams.

By this time, Wallis was in full flow in his enthusiasm to sell the idea. During the morning of 28 January, he showed a film of the Chesil Beach trials at Vickers House in London to key figures in Vickers and the Air Ministry. Two days later, he sent a copy of his paper 'Air Attack on Dams' to Lord Cherwell, with a long covering letter in which he described it as a report on:

> the effect of destroying the large barrage dams in the Ruhr Valley, with some account of the means of doing it ... Large scale experiments carried out against similar dams [in fact, only one dam] in Wales have shown that it is possible to destroy the German dams if the attack is made at a time when these are full of water (May or June) ... It is felt that unless the operations made against the dams are carried out almost simultaneously with naval operation, preventative measures will make the dam project unworkable and that therefore the development of the large sphere of five tons weight should be given priorities equal to those of the smaller weapon.

In the event, Wallis made the rash promise that the larger bomb, Upkeep, would be developed within two months. He explained the significance of breaching the dams and concluded:

> In the Ruhr district the destruction of the Möhne Dams alone would bring about a serious shortage of water for drinking purposes and industrial supplies. In the Weser district the destruction of the Eder and

Diemel Dams would seriously hamper transport in the Mitteland Canal and in the Weser, and would probably lead to an almost immediate cessation of traffic.

'THIS IS TRIPE'

This time he received a more favourable reaction from Cherwell, and things began to happen. By mid-February, Sir Arthur 'Bomber' Harris was briefed. Initially, Harris did not seem to grasp the difference between Highball and Upkeep, but in any case he dismissed the whole concept with the words:

This is tripe of the wildest description. There are so many ifs & ands that there is not the smallest chance of it working ... I don't believe a word of its supposed ballistics on the surface ... at all costs stop them putting aside Lancasters and reducing our bombing effort on this wild goose chase ... [It is] another Toraplane [a flying torpedo] – only madder. The war will be over before it works – and it never will.

When his aides persisted, Harris became even more vitriolic in his criticism:

I am now prepared to bet that the Highball is just about the maddest proposition as a weapon that we have yet come across – and that is saying something ... The job of rotating some 12,000 lbs of material at 500 rpm on an aircraft is in itself fraught with difficulty. The slightest lack of balance will just tear the aircraft to pieces, and in the packing of the explosive, let alone in retaining it packed in balance during rotation, are obvious technical difficulties ... I am prepared to bet my shirt a) that the weapon itself cannot be passed as a prototype inside six months; b) that its ballistics will in no way resemble those claimed for it; c) that it will be impossible to keep such a weapon in adequate balance either when rotating it prior to release or at all in storage and d) that it will not work, when we have got it ... Finally, we have made attempt after attempt to pull successfully low attacks with heavy bombers. They have been, almost without exception, costly failures ... while nobody would object to the Highball enthusiasts being given one aeroplane and being told to go away and play while we get on with the war, I hope you will do your utmost to keep these mistaken enthusiasts within the bounds of reason and certainly to prevent them from setting aside any number of our precious Lancasters for immediate modification.

'BOMBER' HARRIS

When Harris took over Bomber Command in February 1942 he was immediately forced to defend it. In one of his first letters to Air Chief Marshal Sir Charles Portal, he wrote:

I must bring to your urgent and earnest attention the deplorable effect on morale of the spate of largely ignorant and uninstructed chatter against our bombing policy and against the general efficiency and co-operativeness of the Air Force.

By May, at least the *Daily Express* seemed to be on side, quoting Harris as saying:

If I could send 1,000 bombers to Germany every night, it would end the war by the autumn. We are going to bomb Germany incessantly ... the day is coming when the USA and ourselves will put over such a force that the Germans will scream for mercy.

Harris could not put up 1,000 bombers *every* night, but on 30–31 May he *did* send 1,000 bombers to attack Cologne. This certainly imprinted his name on the consciousness of the British people. At last the press could shout with headlines such as: 'The World's Biggest Air Raid', 'The Greatest Air Raid in History' and 'One Bomber every Six Seconds'.

In spite of Harris's outbursts against Wallis's idea, Air Vice-Marshal the Hon. Ralph Cochrane persuaded him that he should see Wallis, and on 17 February Harris did so at Headquarters Bomber Command, High Wycombe. Harris's greeting to him was: 'What the hell do you damn inventors want? My boys' lives are too precious to be thrown away by you.' Later he would say: 'I was damned if I would have my pilots out-kamikazing the Kamikazes!'

FINAL PREPARATIONS

In fact, Harris had already authorised the conversion of

three Lancasters so that Wallis's weapon could be tested, though he did say that no more would be modified until the tests proved positive. By this time, Sir Charles Portal was completely converted, and said to Harris: 'If you want to win the war bust the dams.'

There were still some setbacks, though, and at one point Wallis offered to resign. However, at a meeting on 26 February 1943 with representatives of the Air Ministry, the Ministry of Aircraft Production, Vickers Armstrong (including the Chairman, Sir Charles Craven), and Roy Chadwick, Wallis was told by Air Vice-Marshal John Linnell that the Chief of Air Staff wanted *every endeavour* to prepare the weapons and aircraft for use in the spring of 1943. Upkeep now had priority over the Windsor at Vickers Armstrong and other Lancaster projects at Avro. Thirty modified Lancasters, three immediately for trials, were to be produced by 1 May. The separation of modifications between Avro and Vickers had not been agreed but, after discussion, it was decided that Avro would handle strongpoint attachments to the airframe, bomb cell fairings, bomb-release electrical wiring and the hydraulic powerpoint for the rotating motor, while Vickers would be responsible for the attachment arms carrying the mine, including the driving mechanism, and the mine itself.

So Wallis had the orders for which he had striven for three years. Furthermore, he also had eight weeks, which he had always said was all he needed. He said later that he felt 'physically sick because somebody had actually called my bluff', and he now realised that he had such a short time for 'the making good of all my claims'.

He still had not completed the final drawings, but did

so by Sunday 28 February. As far as engines were concerned, the Lancaster II with its Bristol Hercules engines was found to be unsuitable, and so Lancaster IIIs with the Rolls-Royce Merlin 22, made under licence by the American firm Packard, were used.

In the opinion of F.W. Winterbotham, Chief of Air Intelligence of the Secret Intelligence Service from 1930 to 1945, the greater impact of German bombs led Barnes Wallis to question why this should be the case. Winterbotham wrote in his book, *Secret and Personal*, published in 1969:

> I suppose it had been principally due to the RAF's policeman-like duties in the Middle East that we had not, in fact, developed a large bomber or a large bomb during the inter-war years. It seemed, therefore, that we knew very little about the effect of bombs of five hundred pounds and upwards. Air Marshal Sir Victor Goddard had for a long time been advocating four-engined bombers to carry larger bombs, but this had never come off. Our bombing in the Middle East had been principally for punitive destruction of Arab villages or anti-personnel bombs and the like. The efficiency of our bombs had therefore been reckoned in blast value. It had evidently been decided, on this basis, that it was better to drop a number of small bombs to create a wider area of destruction by blast than confine the damage to a single large one. The German five-hundred-pound bombs were causing destruction out of all proportion to their blast effect, especially since they usually exploded deep inside a building ...

10. The Wellington bomber on the day of its first flight, 15 June 1936. Mutt Summers, chief test pilot of Vickers, was at the controls, while Wallis and the general manager of Vickers at Weybridge, Trevor Westbrook, were both on board. It immediately gave a performance far superior to its specification, and went on to become an effective and very popular bomber in the first half of the Second World War. Wallis's geodetic system proved itself, and *The Aeroplane* wrote: 'Wellingtons have returned from raids so damaged that they would appear to be about to collapse at any moment. Yet the geodetic structure spreads the loads so well that even though large sections may be shot away the machines have been able to return to their bases.'

11. Wellington Mark Is of 9 Squadron. The Wellington was the backbone of Bomber Command's night raids over Germany in the early years of the war. In the winter of 1941–2 there were no fewer than 21 squadrons of Wellingtons operational within Bomber Command and, in the first 1,000-bomber raids on Cologne in May 1942, over half the aircraft taking part were Wellingtons.

12. The Warwick bomber, which was to succeed the Wellington. While it was being developed, Wallis was pushing his 'big bomb' theory to the authorities, but Sir Henry Tizard made it clear that the Air Ministry was interested in a more versatile bomber. The Warwick was made obsolete by the four-engine bombers such as the Lancaster. Although an order for 150 Warwick B Mark Is was placed in January 1941, only seventeen were completed.

13. The Manchester bomber. By 1936, the government had realised that medium bombers with relatively light bomb loads would not be adequate for the next year. Their answer was P.13/36, a heavy bomber. Handley Page put forward a specification which became the Halifax, and A.V. Roe one which became the Manchester, 69 feet in length, with a 72-foot wing-span, a gross weight of 37,000 lb, a top speed of 330 mph at 15,000 feet, and a service ceiling of 24,000 feet.

14. The Manchester was powered by two Rolls-Royce Vulture engines. However, the Vulture, a replacement for Rolls-Royce's Buzzard engine, needed further development, and after a number of failures (of the 202 Manchesters built, more were lost to engine failure than to enemy action), both Avro and Rolls-Royce decided that it should be replaced by the proven Merlin and that the Manchester would become a four-engined bomber. Nevertheless, before it was effectively abandoned in the summer of 1942, the Manchester did take part in the 1,000-bomber raids on Cologne, Essen and Bremen.

15. A Lancaster bomber prototype. Even before the Manchester flew on operations, Avro's Chief Designer, Roy Chadwick, realised its serious shortcomings and was planning its replacement. He added twelve feet to the wingspan and replaced the two Rolls-Royce Vulture engines with four Rolls-Royce Merlins. One of Chadwick's colleagues said later that he 'showed himself to be a most resourceful and courageous designer, ultimately snatching success from failure in the most ingenious way with a superlatively successful operational aircraft'. 'Bomber' Harris would tell Chadwick's daughter that her father never received the recognition he deserved.

16. The Lancaster bomber Mark I. This is the Lancaster flown by Squadron Leader H.B. Martin DSO, DFC for 617 Squadron. As soon as it flew, everyone realised how good it was, and large production orders were placed. Avro were overwhelmed, and many other companies and sub-contractors were called in to help. The peak of production was reached in August 1944, a month in which 293 aircraft were completed.

17. This shows a Lancaster Mark I carrying Wallis's Grand Slam bomb. Weighing 36,900 lb when empty, the Lancaster was capable of taking off with another 33,000 lb of fuel and bombs – in other words, almost its own weight again. Its massive bomb bay stretched for 33 feet and, unlike in other bombers, was one continuous, uninterrupted space. Of a total of 7,377 Lancasters built, 3,932 were lost in action. They flew a total of 156,000 sorties and dropped 608,612 tons of bombs.

The German bombers had just started dropping those five-hundred-pounders on London and many and curious were the stories of windows and walls being sucked inwards or outwards, roofs caving in and such-like, often in quite a different street from the actual burst of the bomb.

Wallis's scientific brain was beginning to work on this matter and he was determined to find out *why* all these strange things happened. The answer lay in the great efficiency of the anti-submarine depth-charge detonated under water. This did not destroy by means of blast; it did so by means of a shock-wave which was transmitted by the water itself. Nobody (except perhaps the Germans) seemed to have thought that the air, or the ground, could do the same thing.

By mid-April, tests were taking place in Reculver Bay on the north coast of Kent. There were many failures and a few moderate successes. While some tests were taking place at Reculver, others were being carried out elsewhere. At Boscombe Down in Wiltshire there were range and manoeuvrability tests. Tests for spinning were carried out at Brooklands, Weybridge.

At a meeting at Brooklands on 24 April, Wallis insisted to Wing Commander Guy Gibson, chosen to lead the attack, that it was essential to release the bombs at 60 feet at precisely 232 mph. Fortunately, Gibson, a can-do person if ever there was one, agreed that this could be done. Gibson glossed over any problems with the aircrews, describing them in *Enemy Coast Ahead* as the finest in Bomber Command. The reality was somewhat different, as Sweetman pointed out:

By April 13 some crews were still incomplete, although four of the 157 aircrew on strength were surplus to requirement. And of those originally posted in to the squadron, that of Lovell had by now returned to 57 Squadron and been replaced by Sergeant (soon Pilot Officer) Divall's. The manner of Lovell's departure, three weeks after the formation of Squadron X, underlined the rigorous requirements laid down by Gibson: 'the crew did not come up to the standard necessary for this squadron'. Shortly afterwards another crew went for similar reasons. Gibson proposed to replace a Lancaster's navigator to which the pilot objected. He and the entire crew opted to leave 617 Squadron which was thus reduced to 21 crews at April 16.

By the end of April, 617 Squadron had flown over 1,000 hours in training and the crews were operating at 60 feet at 210 mph (instead of 150 feet as originally planned). By this time they were using Eyebrook reservoir, known in all the operation documents as 'Uppingham Lake', which supplied water to the giant Stewarts and Lloyds steel-works in Corby, Northamptonshire. Fitted with targets, this was used to simulate the Möhne Dam, while Abberton reservoir, known as 'Colchester Lake', was used to simulate the Eder. Howden and Derwent reservoirs were used to simulate the Sorpe.

By this time, the aiming device had also been pretty well perfected and, as Sweetman points out, it had nothing to do with the theatre lights on the chorus-line girls as shown in the 1955 film. Interestingly, in his book

Enemy Coast Ahead, Gibson tells the story of the theatre lights, though in his case it's a strip-tease act.

> Mr Lockspicer [actually Lockspeiser, the civilian Director of Research] of MAP paid the SASO [Senior Air Staff Officer] a visit. He said, 'I think I can help you!' His idea was an old one; actually it was used in the last war. He suggested that spotlights should be placed on either wing of the aircraft, pointing towards the water where they would converge at 150 feet. The pilot could see these spots and when they merged into one he would then know his exact height. It all seemed too simple and I came back to tell the boys. Spam's first words were – 'I could have told you that. Last night Terry and I went to see the show at the Theatre Royal and when the girl there was doing her strip-tease act there were two spotlights shining on her. The idea crossed my mind then!'

In reality, a Wing Commander C.L. Dann, the supervisor of aeronautics at Boscombe Down, used calculations based on the width between the sluice towers on the Möhne Dam. He put together a triangular wooden sight, with a peephole at the apex and two nails at the extremities of the base. The bomb-aimer would hold this by a piece of wood attached to the underside of the apex and look through the peephole. When the two nails and the two towers coincided, he released the bomb. Dann and Gibson organised a trial using the two towers of the Derwent Dam, and were happy with results. However, in practice the triangular sight was far from perfect. At low levels, thermals caused severe buffeting and, as the bomb-aimer needed one hand for the bomb-release mechanism, he could not use two hands to steady the new sight. Various crews devised their own methods.

In early May, with about two weeks to go, the Upkeep weapon – now officially referred to as a mine, not a bomb – had still not been dropped successfully from the air. It was not until 11 May that 617 Squadron aircraft dropped inert-filled Upkeep cylinders in Reculver Bay for the first time. Gibson wrote in his log-book for that day: 'Low level Upkeep dropped at 60 ft. Good run of 600 yards.'

On 14 May, after more practice runs, Wallis was able to record that the tests showed the ability of individual crews 'to put stores on the beach with remarkable accuracy'.

CHAPTER FOUR

DAMBUSTERS

THE BASE – SCAMPTON

At 09:00 hours on Saturday 15 May, Assistant Chief of the Air Staff (ACAS) sent a 'most immediate most secret' message to Bomber Command at High Wycombe:

Op. CHASTISE. Immediate attacks 'X', 'Y' and 'Z' approved. Execute at first suitable opportunity.

'X' was the Möhne, 'Y' the Eder and 'Z' the Sorpe.

The message was transmitted to RAF 5 Group headquarters at Grantham, and Air Vice-Marshal Sir Ralph Cochrane, an old friend of Wallis who, by this time, had been promoted to a senior position in Bomber Command, drove from there past Newark and Lincoln to RAF Scampton to tell Gibson that the attack would take place next day, Sunday 16 May.

Situated just north of Lincoln and to the west of the Roman road Ermine Street (known to us as the A1 and to our fathers as The Great North Road), RAF Scampton was first used in the First World War, when it was known as Brattleby. In December 1916, 33 Squadron with FE2 and FE26 aircraft was posted there. Major A.R. Kingsford wrote:

> Our job was night patrols hunting for Zeppelins; my patrol was Spurn Head to the south of Lincoln for three hours duration and we literally froze.

The patrols were also pointless, as the Zeppelins flew at over 18,000 feet and the FE2's ceiling was 12,000 feet.

Once the war was over, all aircraft and personnel were transferred to South Carlton, and the station was closed in 1919. By 1920, all the buildings had been removed and the land was returned to farming.

However, as re-armament began in the 1930s, Brattleby was again selected as a suitable site for an airfield. It opened as RAF Scampton on 27 August 1936, and in October of that year the first flying units arrived – 9 Squadron flying Heyfords and 214 Squadron flying Virginia and Harrow aircraft. Various squadrons and aircraft came and went, but on 3 September 1939, when war was declared, RAF Scampton was ready with two squadrons of fully armed aircraft. These squadrons, flying Hampdens, were fully involved in mine-laying activities, known as 'gardening', over the next three years.

From June to August 1940, attacks were made on the German battleship *Scharnhorst* at Kiel and on the Dortmund-Ems canal. In August, after a raid on the canal, Flight Lieutenant Learoyd of 49 Squadron won the first Bomber Command Victoria Cross. He attacked the canal at 150 feet and, despite being repeatedly hit, nursed his aircraft back to Scampton, where he waited until dawn before landing.

During 1941 and 1942, the squadrons were re-equipped, first with Manchesters and then with the Lancasters that replaced them. Scampton was involved in the three '1,000 bomber' raids of the summer of 1942, on Cologne, Essen and Bremen. There were further comings and goings of squadrons in 1942 and early 1943, until in March 1943 Wing Commander Guy Gibson was instructed by Bomber Command to assemble 21 Lancaster crews at Scampton to carry out one of the most audacious and ultimately famous operations of the war – Operation Chastise.

When the pilots and their crews were gathered at Scampton, Gibson wrote of their first insight into the Mess:

> Within a second a whisky was shoved into my hand and a beer put on the floor for Nigger [Gibson's black labrador]. Then there was a babbling of conversation and the hum of shop being happily exchanged; of old faces; old hands; targets; bases; and of bombs. This was the conversation that only fliers can talk, and by that I don't mean movie fliers. These were real living chaps who had all done their stuff. By their eyes you could see that. But they were ready for more. These were the aces of Bomber Command.

Sweetman would show later that not all the fliers were quite as experienced as Gibson portrayed them in his book.

Gibson then made a speech to the pilots, who were all anxious for more news of why they had been assembled:

You're here to do a special job, you're here as a crack squadron, you're here to carry out a raid on Germany which, I am told, will have startling results. Some say it may even cut short the duration of the war. What the target is I can't tell you. Nor can I tell you where it is. All I can tell you is that you will have to practise low flying all day and all night until you know how to do it with your eyes shut. If I tell you to fly to a tree in the middle of England, then I want you to bomb that tree. If I tell you to fly through a hangar, then you will have to go through that hangar even though your wing tips might hit either side. Discipline is absolutely essential.

As Gibson was writing during the war, it was felt necessary for him not to mention Barnes Wallis by name, and he therefore referred to him as Jeff. If ever there was an inappropriate name for Wallis, it was Jeff! (Gibson clearly did not feel the same constraint when referring to the chief test pilot of Vickers, Mutt Summers. He referred to him as 'Mutt'.) He wrote of Wallis:

Jeff was neither young nor old, but just a quiet, earnest man who worked very hard. He was one of the real back-room boys of whom little can be told until after the war, and even then I'm not sure their full story will be told ... The lights went out in the lab. and a small screen lit up with a flickering motion picture. The title was simple, 'Most Secret Trial Number One'. Then an aeroplane came into view, diving very fast towards the sea in a sort of estuary. When it got to about two hundred feet it levelled out and a huge cylindrical object fell from it rather slowly towards the water. I was amazed; I expected to see the aircraft blown sky high. But when it hit the water there was a great splash and then – it worked. That's all I can say to describe it – just that it worked, while the aeroplane flew over serenely on its way.

Photo reconnaissance of the whole area of the Ruhr continued to take place, and the latest photographs showed no unusual defensive activity on the dams. Over the Saturday and into the Sunday, the Lancasters were loaded with their mines. Wallis and Hew Kilner, senior executive at Vickers, arrived from Weybridge late on Saturday afternoon and joined Gibson to brief the flight commanders.

One unfortunate incident occurred during the Saturday, which some feared was a bad omen for the mission. Gibson's labrador, Nigger, a favourite on the station, ran out into the road, was hit by a motorist and killed.

THE PLANS

The plans were revealed to the aircrews during Sunday as the aircraft were fully prepared by the ground crews. The Lancasters were to fly from Scampton to the target area 'in moonlight at low level' in three waves. The first wave would have three sections, each of three aircraft. They would take off at ten-minute intervals and fly 'the Southern route [across the Scheldt estuary] to the target area and attack TARGET X [the Möhne]'. The attack would continue 'until the Dam has been clearly breached

... it is estimated this might require three effective attacks'. Once X was breached, the remaining aircraft of this wave were to move on to Y (the Eder), 'where similar tactics are to be followed'. Once X and Y had been breached, any aircraft still carrying mines were to move on to Z (the Sorpe).

Meanwhile, the second wave of five aircraft, 'manned by the specially trained crews', would fly 'the Northern route' across the North Sea to the island of Vlieland, then south-east over the Ijsselmeer to join the same route as the first wave to Germany. The third group of six aircraft would act as 'an airborne reserve'. This group would fly the same route as the first wave.

Each wave was to fly at very low level to help avoid detection. On reaching a point ten miles from the target, each section leader – Gibson, Young and Maudslay – would climb to 1,000 feet and liaise with the others as they arrived. Gibson would attack first and then co-ordinate attacks by the others.

No aircraft should be sent to the Eder until the Möhne had been breached. Gibson was allowed two extra aircraft to widen the breach, provided there were three left to attack the Eder. It was emphasised that the crews should not mistake water spilling over the top of the dam after an explosion for a true breach.

The pilot was to be responsible for line, the navigator for height, the bomb-aimer for range and the flight engineer for speed. To allow turbulence from the previous attack to subside, the interval between attacks should be not less than three minutes.

There were, inevitably, many code words:

Pranger — attack on X, i.e. Möhne
Nigger — X breached, divert to Y, i.e. Eder
Dinghy — Y breached, divert to Z, i.e. Sorpe
Mason — all aircraft return to base
Tulip — No. 2 take over at X
Cracking— No. 4 take over at Y
Gilbert — attack last-resort targets as detailed
Goner — release of weapon, with effect of mine
indicated by numbers:
1. — failed to explode
2. — overshot the dam
3. — exploded over 100 yards from the dam
4. — exploded 100 yards from the dam
5. — exploded 50 yards from the dam
6. — exploded 5 yards from the dam
7. — exploded in contact with the dam
8. — no apparent breach
9. — small breach
10. — large breach

The bomber selected for the Dams Raid was the B. Mark III Lancaster, a development of the Lancaster Mark I, of which 23 were adapted to carry and deliver Wallis's mines. They were modified to be able to carry a mine whose gross weight was no less than 9,250 lb, of which 6,600 lb was the main explosive charge. It was designed to be carried beneath the Lancaster by two V-shaped arms. Modifications to the aircraft included the removal of the bomb doors to mount the gear for the rotating mine, and, to save weight, the omission of the dorsal turret. A small hydraulic motor to drive the rotating gear was installed in the middle section of the cabin. These modifications added 1,000 lb to the all-up weight of the aircraft. Added to the weight of the Upkeep mine itself, this meant that the Lancasters would need every ounce of power from their four Rolls-Royce Merlin engines to get off the ground at Scampton.

The final version of Upkeep was a cylinder approximately 60 inches long and 50 inches in diameter, made of metal three-eighths of an inch thick. It contained 6,600 lb of Torpex underwater explosive compound, three hydrostatic pistols set to explode at 30 feet, and a fourth self-destructive pistol timed to go off 90 seconds after release.

ATTACK – MÖHNE

At 21:39 hours the first wave of three aircraft, led by Wing Commander Gibson, Flight Lieutenant Hopgood and Flight Lieutenant Martin, took off in clear weather with a full moon. After 40 minutes they began crossing a very calm North Sea. The navigators threw out flame floats so that the rear gunners could estimate drift. There was virtually none. Each aircraft tested its spotlights. Stronger winds than anticipated pushed them slightly off course, an error they corrected once over Holland. They encountered no opposition until they reached the Rhine, but from then on were troubled constantly by flak, and Hopgood's port wing was damaged. The later official report stated:

Various small flak posts opened up and as the aircraft flew over a defended area they were caught in the beam of the searchlights while flying at a very low level, but their low level and high speed helped them escape from the searchlights and flak. Several searchlights were shot out of action.

Flight Sergeant Simpson's diary painted a somewhat more haphazard picture:

Lost Hoppy! Later picked up by some searchlights near Rhine – shot some out somewhere – bit off track over some town – bags of shooting – lost Winco – arrived Möhne Hoppy and Winco turned up.

Gibson also admitted later that he had been off course more than once.

As we came over the hill, we saw the Möhne Lake. Then we saw the dam itself. In that light it looked squat and heavy and unconquerable; it looked grey and solid in the moonlight as though it were part of the countryside itself and just as immovable. A structure like a battleship was showering out flak all along its length, but some came from a power house below it and nearby. There were no searchlights. It was light flak, mostly green, yellow and red and the colours of the tracer reflected upon the face of the water in the lake. The reflections on the dead calm of the black water made it seem there was twice as much as there really was ... I scowled to myself as I remembered telling the boys an hour or so ago that they would probably only be the German equivalent of the Home Guard and in bed by the time we arrived.

The second flight of three aircraft, with Squadron Leader Young, Flight Lieutenant Maltby and Flight Lieutenant Shannon in charge, took off eight minutes after the first wave. The final three aircraft, led by Squadron Leader Maudslay, Flight Lieutenant Astell and Pilot Officer Knight, took off after another twelve minutes. Astell did not make it to the dams, crashing between Rees on the Rhine and Dülmen.

Once at the Möhne Dam, Gibson conducted an observation run and then, after reminding Hopgood to take charge if anything happened to him, began his attack run. On came the spotlights to make sure the aircraft was at precisely 60 feet. The mine was dropped at a ground speed of 230 mph. The rear gunner, Trevor-Roper, saw it bounce three times and then a huge sheet of water rose above the dam wall. The water subsided and the wall was still intact. No breach. The message back to HQ was 'Goner 68A' (the Möhne had originally been 'X', but was changed to 'A'), i.e. the mine had exploded 5–50 yards from the dam without breaching.

After a five-minute delay to let the spray clear, Gibson ordered Hopgood in. By this time, the German gunners were fully ready and Hopgood's Lancaster took a lot of flak. As a result, the mine was dropped late and bounced over the dam wall, exploding near the power station and damaging it extensively. The aircraft, severely damaged, struggled up to about 500 feet before exploding. Three of the crew escaped, but only two survived and were taken prisoner.

Gibson then ordered the third aircraft of Martin to attack, and showed the courage that earned him a Victoria

Cross. Gibson flew slightly ahead of Martin, to starboard, to distract the defenders. Martin dropped his mine, but once more the dam was not breached. The message back to Grantham was 'Goner 58A'.

Gibson now called in the fourth Lancaster, this one commanded by Young. Gibson and Martin both carried out manoeuvres to divert the German gunners, and Gibson was delighted to see Young's mine make three good bounces and hit the dam wall exactly as intended. He was sure the wall had been breached, but when the water fell back he could see that it had not. However, he was sure it must have been damaged. Message back – 'Goner 78A'.

Now it was time for the fifth, led by Maltby. Yet again, Gibson and Martin employed diversionary tactics. As Maltby approached, he realised that the dam was already breached. He dropped his mine, which bounced four times, hit the dam wall and exploded. For some reason, even though the dam *was* breached, Maltby's wireless operator sent the message 'Goner 78A'.

Gibson was just telling Shannon to prepare for his attack when he realised the dam was breached:

As he turned I got close to the dam wall and then saw what had happened. It had rolled over, but I could not believe my eyes. I heard someone shout, 'I think she has gone, I think she has gone'. Other voices took up the cry and quickly I said, 'Stand by until I make a recco' … Now there was no doubt about it; there was a great breach one hundred yards across and the water, looking like stirred porridge in the moonlight, was gushing out and rolling into the Ruhr Valley towards the industrial centres of Germany's Third Reich.

Gibson told Shannon not to attack, and instructed his wireless operator to signal 'Nigger'. The seven surviving Lancasters circled to look at the damage. Shannon said later that it was 'almost impossible to describe the elation in success'; Gibson wrote: 'This was a tremendous sight, a sight which probably no man will ever see again.'

Back at Grantham in 5 Group headquarters there was also great elation. Wallis and Cochrane had seen most of the aircraft off at Scampton before driving over to join Harris, Group Captain H.V. Satterley, Cochrane's Senior Air Staff Officer, and Roy Chadwick with duty staff in the underground operations room at Grantham. As each message came in, there was great expectation followed by slumps of despair as it was realised that the dams remained intact. When the message 'Nigger' came through, Satterley remembered that he saw Wallis leap in the air pumping both arms. Harris said to Wallis: 'I didn't believe a word you said when you came to see me. But now you could sell me a pink elephant.'

ATTACK – EDER

However, elation among the aircrews was short-lived, as they realised they must now turn their attention to the Eder Dam. Martin and Maltby set off back to England while those with mines – Shannon, Maudslay and Knight – as well as Gibson himself and Young, who would act as leader if necessary, moved on to the Eder.

Finding the Eder proved quite difficult with the tree-lined banks shrouded in early morning mist. When they eventually found it, they realised that getting into position for a run at the dam was going to be considerably more difficult than they had been led to believe at the briefings. They would have to dive from about 1,000 feet over Waldeck Castle, execute a tight port turn, crossing a small spit of land, and then settle at 60 feet for the final approach. At least there was no flak. The dam was protected only by two sentries armed with rifles.

Shannon went first, but flew over the dam three times without releasing his mine. He was finding it impossible to achieve the correct height after the steep dive and tight turn. Then Maudslay tried twice with no greater success. After Shannon made two more dummy runs, he finally felt confident enough of his position to release his mine. It bounced twice before hitting the dam, causing the usual upsurge but no breach. Maudslay then made a run, but he dropped his mine too late and it hit the parapet.

Now it was Knight's turn and, after one dummy run, he released his mine, which bounced three times before hitting the dam wall slightly right of centre. Once they had climbed to safety, Knight reported:

Large breach in wall of dam almost 30 feet below top of dam, leaving top of dam intact. Torrent of water pouring through breach caused tidal wave almost 30 feet high half a mile down valley from the dam.

Gibson also described the structure 'collapsing as if a gigantic hand had pushed a hole through cardboard'.

Kellow, Knight's wireless operator, said later:

> When we passed over the dam wall at the Eder we
> had to clear a large hill directly ahead of us. After
> the mine had dropped Les [Knight] pulled the nose
> up quite steeply in order to clear this hill and in
> doing so I could look back and down at the dam
> wall. It was still intact for a short while, then as if
> some huge fist had been jabbed at the wall a large
> almost round black hole appeared and water gushed
> as from a large hose.

The rest of the crew were too busy concentrating on
missing the hill to enjoy the sight of the breached dam. As
Sergeant Johnson, the bomb-aimer in Flight Lieutenant
McCarthy's plane, put it:

> The recovery from low level as the bomb was
> released to clear the large hill immediately facing the
> dam wall was quite hair-raising and required the
> full attention of the pilot and engineer to lay on
> emergency power from the engines and a climbing
> attitude not approved in any of the flying manuals
> and a period of nail-biting from the rest of us, not
> least me who was getting too close a view of the
> approaching terra firma from my position in the
> bomb-aimer's compartment.

Once more there was elation, both amongst the crews
and back at Grantham. Harris telephoned Washington,
where he spoke to the Chief of the Air Staff, Sir Charles
Portal.

For Gibson and company, the immediate priority was not to wallow in their success but to get back to Scampton without delay.

Maltby and Martin, who had flown back directly from the Möhne, arrived home almost without incident. Shannon also made it back without any trouble, as did Gibson and Knight. However, neither Maudslay nor Young got home, both being shot down.

ATTACK – SORPE AND ENNEPE

The second wave, which actually left Scampton before Gibson, was briefed to attack the Sorpe Dam. The first aircraft, piloted by Flight Lieutenant Barlow, crashed – probably shot down. Its Upkeep mine did not explode, however, and the Germans would therefore soon be able to examine Wallis's weapon.

The second, piloted by Flight Lieutenant Munro, was badly damaged by flak. Howarth, the front gunner, wrote later:

Badly damaged ... the intercom had been put out of action, also our VHF for communication with the other aircraft in the wave; the master unit for our compass was destroyed and ... the tail turret pipes were damaged. This meant we could not speak to each other in the plane – essential for calling out height and speed and direction in case of fighter attack. We could not speak to the other planes in the wave, and were left with one unreliable compass, and very little defence against fighters. By the time the damage was assessed, we were well into the

Zuider Zee, and our pilot Les Munro decided we had little chance of success if we went on, and decided to turn for home.

The next aircraft in this wave, flown by Pilot Officer Byers, was shot down before it reached the Dutch coast. The one following, flown by Pilot Officer Rice, flew so low as he approached the Dutch coast that the aircraft hit the water and dislodged its mine. Rice had no alternative but to return to Scampton.

The final Lancaster of this wave, piloted by Flight Lieutenant McCarthy, made it to the Sorpe, but McCarthy experienced considerable difficulty lining up the aircraft with the dam, as he had to avoid the church in the nearby village of Langscheid. Time and again, the bomb-aimer, Johnson, refused to release their mine because he was not happy with either the line or height of the aircraft in its final approach. It was not until the tenth run that he let the mine go. It exploded against the dam, but caused only a small breach.

The remaining five reserve Lancasters took off uncertain which dams they would be attacking. The first, flown by Pilot Officer Ottley, was shot down over the well-defended railway centre, Hamm. The second, Pilot Officer Burpee's plane, was also shot down.

Of the remainder, the Lancaster piloted by Flight Sergeant Brown reached the Sorpe, but suffered from the same problems that had plagued McCarthy earlier. As with McCarthy, it was on the tenth run that the mine was released. It exploded against the dam wall, but the crew had to report 'no apparent breach'.

The next to attack was the Lancaster piloted by Flight

Sergeant Townsend. He was instructed to attack the Ennepe, the fourth on the list of six possible dam targets. As with McCarthy and Brown at the Sorpe, Townsend found the achievement of satisfactory line extremely difficult, and it was only on the fourth run that their mine was released. However, it exploded 50 yards short of the dam wall and no breach was achieved.

The aircraft piloted by Flight Sergeant Anderson decided to return to Scampton after suffering some damage.

Chapter Five
After the Raid

THE EFFECT OF THE RAID

When the Möhne Dam was breached, 116 million cubic metres of the 132.2 million in the reservoir poured through the gap within twelve hours. The wave crashing through the Möhne valley was about ten metres high, much higher than in the floods of 1890 which had prompted the building of the dam in the first place. Buildings in the valley within 65 kilometres were destroyed, as were bridges up to 50 kilometres. Eyewitnesses said that before the bridges collapsed, the floodwaters were two metres above them.

Throughout the length of the valley, electricity and water supplies were severely affected. The large Möhne generating station and another smaller one were both destroyed. In Neheim-Hüsten, where the Möhne flowed into the Ruhr, there was a great loss of life. By 31 May, 859 bodies (147 Germans, 712 foreign workers) had been recovered, and there were still nearly 200 reported as missing. Many factories in the valley were either destroyed or badly damaged. As many pumping stations were flooded, ironically a shortage of usable water resulted.

Meanwhile, at the Eder the escape of water, at 154.4 million cubic metres of the 202.4 million in the lake, was equally devastating and lasted longer. John Sweetman wrote:

> In some ways the Eder attack was more far-reaching than that at the Möhne. Heavy flooding of valuable agricultural land and silting-up of irrigation, pumping and electricity supply facilities occurred and, moreover, the bed of the Eder river up to its meeting with the Fulda was, in the words of a later German estimate, 'devastated' … the floods also immobilised four power stations close to the reservoirs … The effect of the floodwater was indeed extensive. Between Gunterhausen and Hannover-Münden the sluices of several small lakes were silted up and suffered structural damage. 30,000 cubic metres of earth had to be dredged from the Fulda and 5,000 cubic metres from the Weser beyond Hannover-Münden to restore navigable channels to normal.

Reaction at the very top of the Third Reich was swift. Albert Speer, Minister of Armament and War Production, was in no doubt that the bombers 'had tried to strike at our whole armaments industry by destroying the hydroelectric plants of the Ruhr'. This is how he described the effects of the raid in his book, *Inside the Third Reich*, written while he was serving his twenty years in Spandau Prison for war crimes:

> The report that reached me in the early hours of the morning was most alarming. The largest of the

dams, the Möhne dam, had been shattered and the reservoir emptied. As yet there were no reports on the three other dams. At dawn we landed at Werl Airfield, having first surveyed the scene of devastation from above. The power plant at the foot of the shattered dam looked as if it had been erased, along with its heavy turbines.

A torrent of water had flooded the Ruhr Valley. That had the seemingly insignificant but grave consequence that the electrical installations at the pumping stations were soaked and muddied, so that industry was brought to a standstill and the water supply of the population imperiled. My report on the situation, which I soon afterward delivered at the Führer's headquarters, made a 'deep impression on the Führer. He kept the documents with him.'

The British had not succeeded, however, in destroying the three other reservoirs. Had they done so, the Ruhr Valley would have been almost completely deprived of water in the coming summer months. At the largest of the reservoirs, the Sorpe Valley reservoir, they did achieve a direct hit on the centre of the dam. I inspected it that same day. Fortunately the bomb hole was slightly higher than the water level. Just a few inches lower – a small brook would have been transformed into a raging river which would have swept away the stone and earthen dam. That night, employing just a few bombers, the British came close to a success which would have been greater than anything they had achieved hitherto with a commitment of thousands of bombers. But they made a single mistake which puzzles me to this day: They divided their forces and that same night destroyed the Eder Valley dam, although it had nothing whatsoever to do with the supply of water to the Ruhr.

A few days after this attack seven thousand men, whom I had ordered shifted from the Atlantic Wall to the Möhne and Eder areas, were hard at work repairing the dams. On September 23, 1943, in the nick of time before the beginning of the rains, the breach in the Möhne dam was closed. We were thus able to collect the precipitation of the late autumn and winter of 1943 for the needs of the following summer. While we were engaged in rebuilding, the British air force missed its second chance. A few bombs would have produced cave-ins at the exposed building sites, and a few fire bombs could have set the wooden scaffolding blazing.

Wallis agreed with Speer. He was frustrated by the fact that Bomber Command did not try to stop the reconstruction work on the dams.

At Dortmund on 18 May, Speer met officials responsible for water, gas and electricity supplies and sent a summary of his plans to Hitler. He brought in electrical experts from all over Germany and made it their top priority to restore water and electrical supply in the stricken area, regardless of harmful effects elsewhere. According to Sweetman:

Forty-eight hours after the raid, with Hitler's approval, 7,000 workers were on their way to help in the clearing-up process and to prepare for the

necessary rebuilding in the administrative areas of
the Möhne valley, Eder valley, Dortmund and
Kassel, and a further 20,000 were to concentrate as
soon as possible; many of these were withdrawn
from the Atlantic Wall. Such was the gravity of the
situation, Speer noted, that this was the only time
that Todt Organisation labourers were employed
within Germany rather than in occupied countries,
and construction overseers were appointed to super-
vise the various repair projects. [Organisation Todt
was a construction and engineering group created
by Fritz Todt which carried out many large construction projects for the Nazis, including the Atlantic
Wall and the Gustav Line in Italy. It was made up
of a small group of technical advisors and a huge
number of foreign workers – 1.5 million by 1944. In
1942, following Todt's death, it came under Speer's
control.] Worried about drinking water, Speer ordered
preparation of a special report about the supply
and distribution of domestic water supplies, which
would take into account associated drainage as well.

Speer returned to Berlin on 20 May and told Joseph
Goebbels, the Propaganda Minister, that the damage was
not as bad as he had feared at first. He hoped that the
armaments industry would be back in full working order
within days. Goebbels recorded in his diary: 'Speer is
truly a management genius.' As for Hitler, the raid clearly
rattled him. In talking to Field Marshal Keitel and Major
General Warlimont on 19 May, he referred to 'this disaster
in the West', and went on to reply to Warlimont's comment that the impact was not severe:

That may be so in the summer months. If a dry year occurs, it will be 'catastrophic'. If we encounter a year when the Ruhr has no water, can we survive?

According to Goebbels, Hitler was furious at the Luftwaffe's failure to prevent the attack.

Certainly, some of the foreign press got hold of the story. On 18 May, the *New York Times* quoted 'a telegram from Berne' to report that the German public was now apprehensive about air raids and that civil unrest had broken out because of the disaster. Morocco Radio reported rioting in Duisburg and Dortmund. Reuters' correspondent in Stockholm, Bernard Valery, claimed that the damage would take 'at least six months to repair', and their man in Zürich, Reginald Langford, reported that morale in Kassel was at a low ebb.

'THE FINEST TECHNICAL ACHIEVEMENT OF THE WAR'

In Britain, the press and radio spent 17 May broadcasting the news – this was how the wives of both Wallis and Gibson learnt of their husbands' achievements. Official reaction was, of course, positive. At 8:30 a.m. on 17 May, Cochrane sent a personal message to Gibson:

All ranks in 5 Group join me in congratulating you and all in 617 Squadron on a brilliantly conducted operation. The disaster which you have inflicted on the German war machine was a result of hard work, discipline and courage. The determination not to be beaten in the task and getting the bombs exactly on the aiming point in spite of opposition has set an example others will be proud to follow.

Later that day, the Secretary of State for Air, Sir Archibald Sinclair, also sent a congratulatory letter to 'Bomber' Harris. Portal in Washington sent a telegram:

Heartiest congratulation to you [Harris] and all Bomber Command on the outstanding recent successes against Germany. In particular please tell the special Lancaster unit of my intense admiration for their brilliant operation against German reservoirs last night.

Portal also wrote to Wallis on behalf of the Royal Air Force:

No small part of the credit for what the RAF has been able to do goes to you ... Thank you for all your efforts on our behalf.

Sir Hugh Trenchard wrote:

Many congratulations on destruction of dams; it is splendid. Please congratulate Gibson and all concerned from me. Wonderful work of Bomber Command is being recognised by all now.

And Cochrane did not forget Wallis:

Before reaching the end of this somewhat long but exciting day I felt I must write to tell you how much

I admire the perseverance which brought you the astounding success which was achieved last night. Without your determination to ensure that a method which you knew to be technically sound was given a fair trial we should not have been able to deliver the blow which struck Germany last night.

Stafford Cripps, Cabinet Minister, wrote to Wallis from the Ministry of Aircraft Production:

I should like to take the earliest opportunity of expressing to you the thanks of His Majesty's Government for the prolonged and distinguished work that you have carried out in perfecting the devices which were used with such devastating success to destroy the Ruhr dams.

I was instructed last night by the War Cabinet to convey to you their high appreciation of this great contribution to our victory.

Harris also sent a telegram to Wallis:

We in Bomber Command in particular and the United Nations as a whole owe everything to you in the first place for the outstanding success achieved.

A letter was also received from Roy Chadwick, Chief Engineer of A.V. Roe, dated 25 May 1943:

I have intended to write to you ever since, but I have been waiting anxiously to hear of some official recognition of the wonderful work that you have done. I am very disappointed not to have heard of any reward for you. It is incredible that your name has not been mentioned in connection with the Dam busting exploit and the only reason I can think of is that some authority imagines that it would give away the secret, or perhaps they think the Gestapo might abduct you!

Guy Gibson wrote to Wallis:

All my pilots and I are honoured that we had the opportunity to take part in the last great experiment which has proved all your theories.

Wallis was particularly pleased with a letter from his long-time supporter, Sir Henry Tizard:

Taking it all in all, from the first brilliant ideas, through the model experiments and the full scale trials, remembering also that when the sceptics were finally convinced you had to work at the highest pressure to get things done in time, I have no hesitation in saying that yours is the finest technical achievement of the war.

From Mary, Wallis's elder daughter, by this time aged 17, who had taken part in the marble experiments, came a telegram from her boarding school near Salisbury: 'HOORAY WONDERFUL DADDY.'

Chadwick wrote:

It was a great pleasure for me to have helped you in some small measure and I shall always remember this particular operation as an example of how the Engineers of this country have contributed substantially towards the defeat of our enemies.

To which Wallis replied:

To you personally, in a special degree, was given the making or breaking of this enterprise for if at that fateful meeting in CRD's [Controller of Research and Development, Ministry of Aircraft Production] office of the 26th February, you had declared the task impossible of fulfilment in the given time, the powers of opposition were so great that I should never have got instructions to go ahead. Possibly you did not realise how much hung on your instantaneous reaction, but I can assure you that I very nearly had heart failure until you decided to join the great adventure. No one believed that I should do it. You yourself said it would be a miracle if we did, and I think the whole thing is one of the most amazing examples of team work and co-operation in the whole history of war.

In replying to Air Vice-Marshal Cochrane, Wallis wrote:

It is impossible to find words adequately to express what one feels about the air crews. The gallantry with which they go into action is incomparable. While the older generation of Air Force officers may not be called upon to carry out actual attacks in person, the spirit of their juniors must proceed from their thought and training, and in praising your crews I would like to add the thanks which I feel are due to you as one of the senior officers of the Air Force, for the outstanding generation of pilots which your example and training has produced. Will you please accept the deepest sympathy of all of us on the losses which the Squadron has sustained. You will understand, I think, the tremendous strain which I felt at having been the cause of sending these crews on so perilous a mission, and the tense moments in the Operation Room when, after four attacks, I felt that I had failed to make good, were almost more than I could bear; and for me the sub-sequent success was almost completely blotted out by the sense of loss of those wonderful young lives. In the light of our subsequent knowledge I do hope that all those concerned will feel that the results achieved have not rendered their sacrifice in vain.

Wallis struggled for the rest of his days with remorse about the loss of life on the Dams Raid, and whenever the subject was raised, he said that he did not want to talk about it.

In describing the raid, the tabloid press were as prone to exaggeration as ever. The *Daily Express* wrote:

Meanwhile Gibson flew up and down alongside the dam to draw the fire of the light anti-aircraft guns emplaced on it. Guns were poking artfully con-cealed out of the slots in the walls.

The *Daily Mail* showed a map of the area supposedly 'devastated', which included most of the industrial Ruhr from Hamm to Düsseldorf and Duisburg to Soest.

18. Wing Commander Guy Gibson DSO and Bar, DFC and Bar (right), who led 617 Squadron on the Dams Raid. In his book *Enemy Coast Ahead*, Gibson described his aircrews as the finest in Bomber Command. Writing during the war within strict security guidelines, he was forced to use code words for a number of key elements in the raid. For example, he called Wallis 'Jeff' and wrote: 'Jeff was neither young nor old, but just a quiet earnest man who worked very hard.'

19. Guy Gibson leads his crew into their Lancaster, specially adapted to carry one of Wallis's dambusting mines, before their aircraft led 617 Squadron on the Dams Raid.

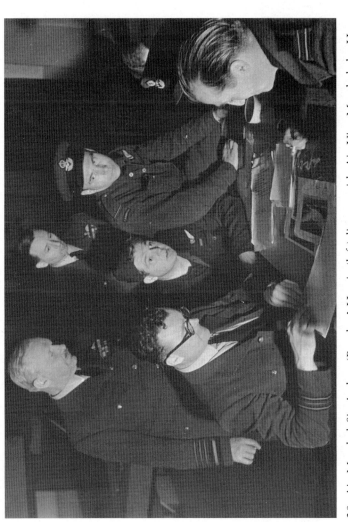

20. Air Marshal Sir Arthur 'Bomber' Harris (left) listens with Air Vice-Marshal the Hon. Ralph Cochrane (standing at back) to the debriefing of a crew member after the Dams Raid.

21 and 22. King George VI meets the Dambusters. King George and Queen Elizabeth visited Scampton after the Dams Raid, and here he is seen congratulating Wing Commander Gibson as they examine photographs taken by Spitfires which showed the extensive damage caused by the breaching of the dams. Gibson was awarded the Victoria Cross for his outstanding bravery in the raid, during which he deliberately drew flak on to his aircraft while others made their attacks on the Möhne Dam.

23. Air Vice-Marshal the Hon. Ralph Cochrane (in uniform) greets Sir Archibald Sinclair, the Secretary of State for Air. Cochrane had always been in favour of precision bombing and was therefore a supporter of Wallis's ideas. As AOC (Air Officer Commanding) 5 Group, he supervised the Dams Raid. Sinclair, an old friend of Prime Minister Winston Churchill, was also in favour of precision bombing on key industrial targets in Germany.

24. Möhne Dam breach damage. As well as the damage to German industrial production in the Ruhr valley after the Dams Raid, one of the other benefits was the raising of morale in Britain and in German-occupied countries in Europe. The RAF took thousands of photographs showing the damage and distributed them to the press in Britain and the USA, as well as including them in leaflets dropped in the occupied territories. This photograph shows Fröndenberg-Bösperde in the Ruhr valley, thirteen miles from the breached Möhne Dam, with various damaged installations:

1. Submerged road
2. Isolated electricity works
3. Destroyed road bridge
4. Destroyed railway bridge
5. Wrecked railway coaches
6. Submerged railway sidings

25. The Eder Dam breached. This shows the south-east end of the Eder Lake, with the dam breached between the two valve houses. The breach measures about 180 feet at the crown of the dam.

26. The effect on the town of Kassel. This photograph shows the damage to the industrial town of Kassel, about 30 miles downstream of the Eder Dam. With its population of 200,000, Kassel was an important centre of production for aircraft, locomotives and U-boat engines.

The language was lurid, the 'facts' somewhat stretched:

Two mighty walls of water were last night rolling irresistibly down the Ruhr and Eder valleys. Railway bridges, power stations, factories, whole villages and built-up areas were being swept away … No man-made defence can stand in their way … It is quite impossible to predict where the damage will end … the devastation done to Germany's war machine has probably only just begun.

Winston Churchill was able to use the success of the raid in his speech to the US Congress on 19 May, saying:

The condition to which the great centres of German war industry, and particularly the Ruhr, are being reduced is one of unparalleled devastation. You have just read of the destruction of the great dams which feed the canals and provide the power to the enemy's munitions works. That was a gallant operation, costing eight out of the nineteen Lancaster bombers employed, but it will play a very far-reaching part in reducing the German munition output … Wherever their centres [for war industry] exist or are developed, they will be destroyed.

A CONJURING TRICK

Inevitably, there were those who claimed that the Dams Raid was unimportant and had little effect on Germany's ability to carry on its war effort. As Sweetman notes:

One British journalist wrote: 'The truth about the Dams Raid is that it was a conjuring trick, virtually devoid of military significance ... The story of the raid is one of sloppy planning, narrow-minded enthusiasm and misdirected courage.' In *New Scientist* an academic scientist argued: 'The dams raid ... had scant effect on German war production; the influence of the ricochet bomb on the imponderable sum of war was negligible.' At virtually the same time, in Germany, publishers of a book about the operation claimed that 617 Squadron's efforts '... were given publicity abroad far in excess of their significance – after the war an elaborate legend has been built upon them.' A separate German commentator maintained that the attack on the Möhne was 'not worth a single aeroplane to breach this dam for the effect it had on the German war effort.'

Sweetman gives details of the installations that were quickly back in action: water supplies in Neheim and Wickede, and the output of water in the Ruhr area; and he notes that there was 'No need to rebuild electricity stations at the Möhne and Herdecke.' He also shows that Albert Speer's ministry produced figures showing that output of aircraft, ammunition and weapons in the third quarter of 1943 exceeded that of the second quarter, and continued to rise in 1944. Steel production in Greater Germany and the Nazi-occupied countries was two-and-a-half million tons higher in 1943 than in 1942.

However, Sweetman also shows that there was some serious damage: 'The waterworks at Fröndenberg and Echthausen were not restored to full working order until

August 1943.' And the Ruhr '*did* suffer a loss of eight per cent of steel output in the second half of 1943.' There was also some heavy damage to agriculture, mainly through the washing away of topsoil and, by mid-1943, Germany's food supplies were beginning to come under strain so that *any* loss of crops or livestock was cumulatively damaging.

As for the dams themselves, as we have seen, the Möhne was repaired by late September. Indeed, Speer and other officials flew to a special celebration there on 2 October. The Eder's repair was completed at about the same time.

This is the view of Peter Calvocoressi, Guy Wint and John Pritchard in their book *Total War*:

> Precision bombing remained impossible except at ruinous cost. When in May 1943 the Möhne, Eder and Sorpe dams were breached in an attempt to immobilise industry in the Ruhr (by dispersing the waters stored to provide energy for industry) the attack was made from the perilous height of 60 feet by a select band of 19 Lancasters carrying a specially designed mine and crews who had been trained for months over replicas of the target area. Eight of the 19 aircraft were lost, 54 of 133 men killed. This heroic operation had been conceived before the war but rejected, and its outcome justified that rejection in as much as it proved to be horribly costly and only moderately successful. Six dams were attacked, two were breached [in the event, only four dams were attacked; the final two, the Lister and the Diemel, were reserves and were not targeted in the

raid]; a number of German workers were drowned but the German grid was able to prevent serious industrial disruption. The air weapon was still at the stage of the bludgeon; precision bombing was suicidal. No comparable raid was ever carried out. The bombing of cities remained Bomber Command's main way of proving the claim of air-power to be a war-winner, the civilian population being the principal target with factories as, in the words of a Bomber Command directive, a bonus.

GREAT FOR MORALE

Morale is a very important factor in war, and much was given by both sides to boosting the morale of their own forces and civilians and lowering that of the enemy's.

In looking at the effect of the Dams Raid on German morale, we have to consider both the raid itself and the effect of the continuous bombing of Germany. The German writer Hans Rumpf pointed out that the raid would have damaged the morale of the local German population because it made the authorities and the Luftwaffe appear incompetent in not being able to defend the dams.

Bomber Command had its own resident BBC correspondent, Richard Dimbleby (later to become perhaps the Corporation's most famous current affairs correspondent). Harris gave Dimbleby free rein, telling his personal assistant:

Mr Dimbleby can talk to anyone he likes, go where he likes, and see anything he likes, and be directly responsible to me.

Dimbleby it was who passed on to the world Harris's message to the crews returning from the Dams Raid:

> Your skill and determination in pressing home the attack will for ever be an inspiration to the RAF. In this memorable operation you have won a major victory in the Battle of the Ruhr, the effects of which will last until the Boche is swept away in the flood of final disaster.

Whether the Dams Raid made a huge impact on German output or not, it certainly prompted fear that the effect on German morale would be damaging. On 23 May 1943 the *Westdeutscher Beobachter*, describing Harris's cold, brutal features, wrote:

> How eagerly he launches his bombs against German women and children to the accompaniment of most unmilitary speeches and articles in which he expresses his grim satisfaction in the doing of it. He is the right man to fight against those who have no defence ... they have small and miserable minds who plan and carry out such undertakings ... Harris may be a savage, he may be the best man for the job, but in him one sees the means to which England, so old and once so proud, is reduced in the fight for existence.

Goebbels was also clearly worried, and his newspaper, *Das Reich*, wrote:

> His parents had no social standing, he lacked any

trace of culture or respect for the cultural achievements of other countries, and his Air Force career, though it had provided wide experience, had been undistinguished. Then, when England chose to intensify the bombing offensive in preference to fairer and more open methods of war, the unscrupulousness of his methods and his harsh treatment of those beneath him were naturally a recommendation.

The Allies, of course, used the raid to all possible good effect. Photographs of the breached dams were circulated as widely as possible, and leaflets including the photographs were dropped in occupied France and the Netherlands. At home, many spoke or wrote of the 'tremendous uplift' they felt at the news.

Elizabeth Stebbing, who worked in MI6, wrote later:

The day after the raid when I saw the first photographs of this river of water rushing through the heart of Germany was the first time that I ever remember Intelligence getting excited because we had done something which had been considered quite impossible.

Micky Martin, a very important member of one of the crews, recalled:

The effect of the dams raid on the public morale was tremendous. It seemed to catch their whole imagination. And it was proof, too, of a cohesion, so necessary in war, where you have to tie together so many threads of human activity. It starred the brilliant scientist Barnes Wallis and his inventions, and coupled with them the exceptional organising power and drive of Sir Arthur Harris and ... the brilliant leadership of a young man, Guy Gibson.

And this showed the British public that from every quarter and every section they could get together for really clouting the Nazis and winning the war.

CHAPTER SIX

TALLBOY AND GRAND SLAM

THE END OF UPKEEP

The effect on Wallis's reputation and on that of 617 Squadron was extremely positive. The squadron had been formed for a specific task, but it now stayed together to carry out raids on the German battleship *Tirpitz* and on the Krebs barrage. It also developed, under the inspirational leadership of Wing Commander Leonard Cheshire, a low-level marking technique which increased dramatically the accuracy of night-bombing.

As we saw, 'Bomber' Harris had been extremely sceptical of, and downright rude to, Wallis, but he now referred to him as 'a wizard boffin'. Wallis himself wrote that:

[Operation Chastise] tended to establish in the minds of C-in-Cs such as Sir Arthur Harris and the CE [Chief Executive of the Ministry of Aircraft Production] Sir Wilfrid Freeman, an impression of the rightness of the lines on which I argued when writing my 'Notes on means of Attacking'.

The possibilities of the spinning bomb for anti-shipping

had not been overlooked in Britain, nor indeed in Germany. Professor Wagner at Junkers had done work on spinning bombs since 1940. As well as 617 Squadron, 618 Squadron of Coastal Command had been formed on 1 April 1943 to operate Mosquitos using a variant of Wallis's bomb, the Highball.

Smaller than Upkeep, Highball worked on the same principle. Spun backwards at up to 1,000 rpm, it bounced across the water until striking its target. After rebounding, it spun forwards again under the ship, where it was exploded by means of a hydrostatic fuse. A 600-lb explosive charge was contained in Highball, and the Mosquito could carry two in tandem in the bomb bay with the doors removed.

Development, including dropping trials, was carried out by Vickers during April 1943. The flying was done from Manston in Kent, mostly by Shorty Longbottom. Trials continued through the summer of 1943, and it was not until the spring of 1944 that various problems were overcome. By this time, the German fleet was not seen as a priority target, and 618 Squadron was sent to the Far East to join carrier-based operations against the Japanese.

However, by the time the squadron arrived, no satisfactory role could be found for it, and in July 1945 its Highballs were destroyed in Australia. Experimental work continued until 1947, when it was quietly dropped.

Although Harris had promised Wallis that he would receive a knighthood, he had to settle for being made a Commander of the British Empire. He must have been further disappointed by Bomber Command's failure to follow up the successful raids on the Ruhr dams.

Although he drew up a list, which included several hundred possible targets not only in Germany and Italy, but also in Holland, France and Romania, the bomb was not used against dams again.

There were several discussions on how to follow up Chastise using similar techniques, and Wallis himself was very keen to attack Italian dams. Nevertheless, he did appreciate that their configuration was different and therefore that more research would be necessary. However, the Upkeep mines were never used again and, after the remaining mines were dumped in the Atlantic, the specially modified Lancasters were scrapped.

Jack Morpurgo suggested in his biography of Wallis that it was because of both the danger to the crews and the emphasis on Wallis's other bombs that Bomber Command eschewed further use of the dams technique. He wrote:

> The nearest one can come to verifiable evidence for the reasoning that lay behind this attenuated history is based upon a letter from Sir Arthur Harris to the author of this biography in which the Commander-in-Chief implies that as the Dams Raid had reinforced his long-held respect for Wallis, as he knew already at the time of the Raid that Wallis had in mind other and even more potent weapons, and as all Wallis weapons were likely to make substantial demands upon the courage and skill of air-crews, he decided to reserve 617 Squadron for the delivery of future Wallis bombs.

As Morpurgo points out, there's a weakness in this

argument, because 617 Squadron completed other missions before the new Wallis bombs were ready. More likely, and again Morpurgo highlights this, is that Allied intelligence was already feeding back information on new weapons being developed by the Germans, and that Wallis's big bombs and the delivery of them on specific targets might be more important than hitting some of the less decisive targets in Wallis's long list.

THE NEW THREAT

The new German weapons were, of course, the un-manned rocket and the flying bomb, the V-1 and V-2. Wallis was told officially about them at the Air Ministry on 12 July 1943. Intelligence had long suspected the existence of these weapons, but by this time there was no doubt, and a special committee was set up under Duncan Sandys, Parliamentary Secretary to the Ministry of Supply, to ascertain the truth regarding the existence and visibility of the weapons, and to suggest possible counter-measures. By this time, too, there was no doubting how seriously everyone was taking the potential threat, because this committee was instructed to report directly and solely to the Cabinet.

Peenemunde, at the mouth of the River Peene on Germany's Baltic coast, had been identified as the centre for experimenting with these weapons, and local intelligence fed back the information that the Germans were well advanced in their development and production. Furthermore, the realisation quickly dawned that there was no defence against them. Stopping bombers was one thing, and had been achieved – just – in the long hot summer of 1940, but unmanned rockets packed with explosives was another, frightening matter.

This was Albert Speer's view of Hitler's plans for the V-2 rocket:

Hitler now decided to use our big new rockets to retaliate against England. From the end of July 1943 our tremendous industrial capacity was diverted to the huge missile later known as the V-2: a rocket forty-six feet long and weighing more than thirteen metric tons. Hitler wanted to have nine hundred of these produced monthly.

The whole notion was absurd. The fleets of enemy bombers in 1944 were dropping an average of three thousand tons of bombs a day over a span of several months. And Hitler wanted to retaliate with thirty rockets that would have carried twenty-four tons of explosives to England daily. That was the equivalent of the bomb load of only twelve Flying Fortresses.

I not only went along with this decision on Hitler's part but also supported it. That was probably one of my most serious mistakes. We would have done much better to focus our efforts on manufacturing a ground-to-air defensive rocket. It had already been developed in 1942, under the code name Waterfall, to such a point that mass production would soon have been possible, had we utilised the talents of those technicians and scientists busy with rocket development at Peenemunde under Wernher von Braun.

On the morning of July 7, 1943, Professor C.

Krauch, the commissioner for chemical production, told me that he had invited Dornberger and von Braun to headquarters at Hitler's request. The Führer wanted to be informed on the details of the V-2 project. After Hitler had finished with one of his conferences, he had gone over to the movie hall, where some of Wernher von Braun's assistants were ready. After a brief introduction the room was darkened and a colour film shown. For the first time Hitler saw the majestic spectacle of a great rocket rising from its pad and disappearing into the stratosphere. Without a trace of timidity and with a boyish sounding enthusiasm, von Braun explained his theory. There could be no question about it: From that moment on, Hitler had been finally won over. Dornberger explained a number of organisational questions, while Krauch proposed to Hitler that von Braun be appointed a professor. 'Yes, arrange that at once with Meissner', Hitler said impulsively. 'I'll even sign the document in person.'

Apparently Hitler bade the Peenemunde men an exceedingly cordial good-bye. He was greatly impressed, and his imagination had been kindled. Back in his bunker he became quite ecstatic about the possibilities of this project. 'The A-4 is a measure that can decide the war. And what encouragement to the home front when we attack the English with it! This is the decisive weapon of the war, and what is more it can be produced with relatively small resources. Speer, you must push the A-4 as hard as you can! Whatever labour and materials they need must be supplied instantly. You know I was going to sign the decree for the tank programme. But my conclusion now is: Change it around and phrase it so that A-4 is put on a par with tank production. But', Hitler added in conclusion, 'in this project we can use only Germans. God help us if the enemy finds out about the business.'

Knowing that the production and launch centres for such weapons would almost certainly be underground, the British made Wallis's 12,000-lb TALLBOY bomb (Wallis always used capital letters when referring to it in his notes) top priority. Now, Wallis's paper 'A Note on a Method of Attacking the Axis Powers' (actually not just a note, but 60 pages of typed text with 30 descriptive tables and 20 pages of appendices) took on a meaning which had not been apparent to many who had read it when it was first circulated in 1940.

Wallis had realised the power of the shock-wave effect of explosions in water or in the ground, compared with those in the air. This meant that TALLBOY did not need to land exactly on the target – close by, it would still have a devastating effect. Furthermore, bombers and bombing techniques had advanced greatly since 1940, when Wallis first proposed dropping his large bombs from 40,000 feet. By 1943, the Lancaster, with its pressurised cabin and ability to carry heavy bombs – along with improved bomb-aiming techniques – was making Wallis's ideas feasible.

BIG BOMBS COME INTO THEIR OWN

Wallis suffered a great deal of frustration in selling his

idea of big bombs. This was how J.D. Scott, in his official history of Vickers, explained the background:

After Wallis had explained his ideas to him in 1940, Lord Beaverbrook 'asked him to get to work on the big bomber project'.

These moves had a significance beyond the immediate one of initiating work on a big bomber and a big bomb project; their significance lay in the welcoming of a scientist into the higher strategical councils of the Air Force. It was not all to be plain sailing; the project was held up again and again. But for the moment, in July 1940, it seemed to have the necessary blessings … By August 9, only three weeks after the disclosure of the project to Lord Beaverbrook, Wallis was able to visit Sheffield, taking with him preliminary drawings of the bomb casing as he had conceived it. In Sheffield Wallis received enthusiastic co-operation, and the day after he arrived he was able to issue instructions to the Weybridge drawing office about the quality of steel to be used, with full technical details of the design which would have to be observed to make a sound casing for a 10-ton bomb.

Things were going well – too well, for in time of war, with fierce competition for every kind of design and manufacturing capacity, and with many people and institutions deeply convinced that to them and to them alone the methods of winning the war had been revealed, it was inevitable that Wallis's plans should encounter opposition. It was true that he had not only the interest of Lord Beaverbrook, but the backing of Air Marshal Tedder, who was in charge of development in the Ministry of Aircraft Production. But there were also powerful opponents, and the Boards both of Vickers and of the English Steel Corporation understood that in continuing to support the project they were gambling in commodities which in wartime were more valuable than money: time and brains. However, the work went on, and on November 1 the company was able to make proposals to Lord Beaverbrook according to which Vickers would undertake complete responsibility not only for the design of the aircraft to carry a 10-ton bomb, but also for the design and the manufacture of the bomb itself.

From the autumn of 1940 to the summer of 1943, the big bomb project was apparently dead. Bomber Command *was* moving towards bigger bombs – first of 4,000 lb, then two and finally three such bombs joined together – but these were all high-capacity blast bombs, totally different weapons from the remarkable 12,000-lb medium-capacity bomb invented by Wallis.

The revival of Wallis's project began on 12 July 1943, when he was summoned to the Ministry of Aircraft Production to discuss it with Sir Wilfrid Freeman and Sir Ralph Sorbey. They immediately asked him if he remembered his project for a 10-ton bomb. Wallis replied that he did indeed remember it.

'How soon', Freeman asked, 'can you let us have one?' Wallis replied that this would depend entirely upon the priority which Sir Charles Craven would be able to give the project at the English Steel Corporation, whereupon Freeman sent Wallis to ask Craven about this.

A week later, Wallis was once again in conference at Sheffield about the 10-ton bomb. Even now, however, the policy of Bomber Command called for emphasis on the 12,000-lb TALLBOY, a scaled-down version of the 10-ton bomb, drawings for which were quickly produced. A.H. Hird of Vickers, who was then working in the Ministry of Aircraft Production, was asked by Sir Wilfrid Freeman to take responsibility for this project, and Vickers now set to work on the development – which was, and remained, a private venture entered into jointly by Freeman. He was acting on his own personal responsibility, and Vickers were acting on theirs. No contract was drawn up; in fact there were no 'financial arrangements' whatever. Mainly because of the work already done, and the friendly personal relationships that had been established in 1940, developments went extremely smoothly, and TALLBOY bombs were made ready for Air Force use within the space of a few months.

This is Scott's conclusion on the two bombs:

TALLBOY, and its successor Grand Slam, were truly and essentially original weapons, since they combined two hitherto unreconciled qualities, the explosive power of a very large blast bomb, and the penetrating power of what had up to now been reserved for armour-piercing bombs, which, with their thick cases, could not take a large filling of explosive. Falling with a terminal velocity as high as 3,600 feet per second, which was a ballistic achievement of a high order, TALLBOY penetrated earth as though it were butter, and transmitted its devastating shock wave from a great depth.

'Bomber' Harris wrote later of TALLBOY:

> This remarkable bomb was a contradiction in terms; it could penetrate 12 feet of concrete or pierce any ship's armour, but, whereas most armour-piercing bombs have so thick a case that they contain little explosive, this one carried terrific power. It was ballistically perfect and had a very high terminal velocity; it could therefore be aimed with great accuracy.

Wallis's reputation was now such that progress on TALLBOY did not suffer the seemingly interminable delays of his earlier years. By 12 September 1943, there was a prototype available for his inspection. However, it was the scaled-down version weighing 12,000 lb that was used effectively by 617 Squadron in 1944, by which time the squadron was led by Leonard Cheshire.

The first TALLBOYS were dropped on the Saumur railway tunnel on the night of 8–9 June 1944, shortly after the Allied invasion of Normandy. This attack was particularly effective, causing a Panzer division on its way to Normandy by rail to be diverted. This high-precision raid by 617 Squadron, together with aircraft of 83 Squadron, was made with the aid of H₂S radar equipment, and Cheshire dropped his spot flares right into the cutting leading to the tunnel, about 40 yards from its mouth. Many runs were made in order to ensure that the TALLBOY bombs were dropped with accuracy, and while the target was soon obscured by smoke, reconnaissance photographs the next day showed that one bomb had fallen directly on the roof at the entrance to the tunnel, making a crater 100 feet across. Two other bombs had dropped into the cutting, blocking the approach with a 110-foot crater. The Saumur tunnel was never used again until it was cleared by the Allied forces.

Soon afterwards, 617 Squadron was again using TALLBOYS to attack German E-boats at Le Havre and Boulogne. The German response was to launch its new weapon, the flying bomb. Within days, 150 had landed in the south of England, half of them on London. The Chiefs of Staff were placed in a quandary. Should they attack the flying bomb launch sites dispersed throughout northern France or should they support the Allied forces in Normandy? They tried to do both, and on 19 June 1944, 617 Squadron dropped TALLBOYS on V-1 sites at Watten, Wizernes and Rilly-la-Montagne, and on the rocket stores at Siracourt and Creil. Even though the Lancasters were not flying at the height that Wallis had hoped for, the damage was significant. The Germans had to abandon Watten, the tunnels at Wizernes were reduced to rubble, and at Creil and Rilly-la-Montagne the underground shelters collapsed. On 5 July, 617 Squadron attacked Marquise-Mimoyesque, home to another German weapon, a long-range gun, and rendered it virtually unusable.

'Bomber' Harris called the Saumur raid one of the most effective attacks on the approaches to the battlefields of Normandy. He wrote later about Wallis's big bomb in *Bomber Offensive*:

The success of three months' campaign against the railways of North-Western Europe was seen as the two opposing armies began to build their strength in the battlefield. In this the allies were always well ahead of the enemy, and if the railways had been working normally the artificial port which the allies had constructed and their lavish use of ingenious equipment for landing supplies on to the beaches would never have compensated for the immense advantage the enemy would have had from an efficient railway system and interior lines of communication.

Even to move troops and supplies through and round Paris took the enemy several days, and while still far from the battlefield they found the lines blocked as a result of our subsequent bombing of the railways behind the invasion area.

Harris went on to quote an (unnamed) German officer who said after the war:

Your strategic bombing of our lines of communication and transportation resulted in our being unable to move our reserves in time and prevented our troops from ever coming into effective tactical deployment against your forces ... Without this strategic bombing of our lines of communication and transportation, without your gigantic aerial coverage of the landings of your troops, your invasion ships and barges would have been sunk or driven out to sea, and the invasion would have been a dismal failure.

After Wallis's TALLBOY bomb had been used extensively, intelligence units reported back the effects. These are some of the notes put together by Air Commodore C.N.H. Bilney from Headquarters, Bomber Command:

Siracourt – a V-2 storage depot
TALLBOY did a magnificent job on this site by virtually undermining the north-west face of the quarry under the dome, thus breaking up the collar at this point and rendering the dome fully vulnerable to further hits in the same area. This weapon also did useful work in crushing the workings near the south-west corner.

Watten – storage and manufacture of hydrogen peroxide
TALLBOY again proved its worth … The concentration of bombs was so heavy that two out of the six 10-foot square vertical shafts were blocked.

Wizernes – storage and firing point for flying bombs
TALLBOY did a magnificent job by virtually undermining the north-west face of the quarry.

Saumur – key railway tunnel
TALLBOY did a good job on the tunnel.

In April 1945, a team led by Air Vice-Marshal G.A.H. Pidcock and Air Commodore Bilney, and including Barnes Wallis, went on a six-day tour of some of the bombed sites in Germany which had received TALLBOY, Grand Slam and Upkeep bombs. These were the general conclusions:

The results obtained definitely substantiate the claim for deep penetration bombs that they are a first class and, in fact, the only effective weapon for attacking massive masonry or reinforced concrete structures, particularly in soil where deep penetration can be secured ... It is fortunate that targets such as viaducts and bridges are generally situated in valleys where a soft alluvial soil forms an excellent ground for operation of this type of weapon ... Whereas superficial damage can be done to targets of this nature by bombs of medium calibre, such damage results only in temporary dislocation which can be quickly repaired. To cause dislocation over a prolonged period it is essential to use a bomb of sufficient power to destroy a portion or portions of the structure so completely that re-building will become necessary. This extent of damage can be achieved by the use of a relatively small number of these large bombs provided a high degree of accuracy is obtained. The results obtained with these bombs fully justify, on the score of economy of effort, the use of specially trained squadrons for the purpose.

It has been calculated that a total of approximately 2,750 tons of bombs has been aimed at the Bielefeld viaduct. Of this 2,750 tons a total of 150 tons consisted of TALLBOYS and one Grand Slam. All the effective damage to the viaduct was done by two TALLBOYS and one Grand Slam, a total weight of 21 tons.

TIRPITZ

Wallis's bomb was also used against the notorious German battleship *Tirpitz*. 'Bomber' Harris thought that battles at sea between giant battleships had become irrelevant in modern warfare, and wrote scathingly about the Admiralty's obsession with *Tirpitz*:

> During all this period [the second half of 1944] the Admiralty continued to worry about the German navy and in particular, in the autumn of 1944, about the *Tirpitz*; our own battleships with their usual large complement of ancillary craft, were kept hanging about at home in case the Germans should decide to send the poor old lone *Tirpitz* to sea, and it was felt that some use might be found for these large units of the Royal Navy in the Pacific. I was accordingly asked to intervene in this fantastic 'war' between these dinosaurs which both sides had just managed, at great expense and after vast argument, to preserve from their overdue extinction. I was quite willing to do so, but only if this did not seriously interfere with more important operations; I gave an undertaking that we would sink the *Tirpitz* in our spare time.

Harris may have referred to it as 'poor old lone *Tirpitz*', but the fact remained that it was, at 42,000 tons, the largest battleship in western waters for most of the war. It was armed extremely powerfully with eight 15-inch guns, twelve 5.9-inch guns and eighteen 4.1-inch guns. It also had sixteen 37-millimetre and 50 20-millimetre machine guns and 84 anti-aircraft guns. Its armour-plating protection was immense, with side-plates up to 15 inches thick and an 8-inch deck shielding the magazines and engine rooms.

The *Tirpitz* had been stationed in northern waters since January 1942, presumably as a precaution against a possible Allied invasion of Norway. There was no doubting the significance that the Allied leaders placed on its lurking presence. Winston Churchill wrote to his Chiefs of Staff:

> The destruction or even the crippling of this ship is the greatest event at sea at the present time. No other target is comparable to it.

In his book *Enigma: the Battle for the Code*, Simon Sebag-Montefiore confirms the fear and respect which dominated the Allies' view of the *Tirpitz*:

> *Tirpitz* had finally made its first move out of the Baltic, where for a year its crew had been involved in training exercises, on 12 January 1942. For months, Naval Enigma traffic had been telling the British about *Tirpitz*'s state of readiness. Knowing where *Tirpitz* was going was crucial since, wherever it was, it could totally alter the balance of power at sea unless counter-measures were taken swiftly. Although British battleships could just about match *Tirpitz* when it came to fire power, and the ability to carry on floating after being hit by shells, *Tirpitz* was two knots faster. As a result it had the capacity to steam in, destroy a convoy, and then race away

before the British Fleet could bring its own considerable fire power to bear. That was why the Naval Enigma messages concerning the *Tirpitz* were watched so closely.

And it was not only a defensive role against the possible invasion of Norway that the *Tirpitz* was playing. She was also a threat to convoys sent from Britain to her ally the Soviet Union. In March 1942 she sank a straggling merchant navy vessel. In June 1942 the Allies sent two battleships, an aircraft carrier and seven cruisers to protect a Russia-bound convoy. In early July, the *Tirpitz* plus the battle-cruisers *Hipper*, *Scheer* and *Lützow* sailed from Norway, frightening the Allies to such an extent that they ordered their protective ships home, leaving the merchant vessels to fend for themselves. The Germans took fright as well, and scuttled back to Norway. However, their very existence had done the trick, because the convoy was decimated by attacks from U-boats and shore-based aircraft. No fewer than 21 ships were lost, and only 70,000 tons of supplies got through to the Soviet Union.

Jack Morpurgo could not have disagreed more with Harris's view of the irrelevance of the *Tirpitz*:

In the months after the PQ17 [the convoy described above] holocaust almost the whole of the submarine force available to the Allies, large numbers of destroyers, the capital ships of the Home Fleet and sizeable units from the Fleet Air Arm and the Royal Air Force were dedicated to the task of guarding convoys against possible attack by *Tirpitz* and her

companions. The Norwegian Resistance movement, the Royal Navy using manned 'chariot-
torpedoes', and submarines from three Allied navies
all tried unsuccessfully to eradicate the threat
presented by her existence. She survived conventional bomber attacks, protected always by her
heavy anti-aircraft fire-power, her ability to make
smoke, her massive armour-plated deck structure,
by the enveloping mass of the mountains around her
fjord fastness, and by the comparatively minuscular
size of target which she presented to attacking
'planes. The failure of all these attempts contributed
largely to the sensational decision, taken in April
1943, to abandon the Arctic supply route for the
summer months of that year. At just the moment when
the Russians seemed about to destroy the German
armies in the East, and again without firing a shot,
Tirpitz had won a battle of enormous importance.

In September 1944, the *Tirpitz* was hiding in Altenfjord
in north Norway. It was out of range of Lancasters
carrying a normal bomb load, so Harris sent 617 and 9
Squadrons to the Yagodnik base in Russia, with orders to
attack the *Tirpitz* with Wallis's 12,000-lb bombs on their
way back to Britain. Harris hoped that an attack from the
east would take the *Tirpitz* by surprise, and that she
could be effectively bombed before her defensive smoke-
screen could be organised.

The attack was not a complete success, but one
12,000-lb bomb exploded on the bows of the *Tirpitz*,
which damaged but did not sink her. Harris surmised
correctly that she would not be of much use to the enemy

before the war ended, but nevertheless was pressed by the Admiralty to attack her again. The *Tirpitz* had been moved to Tromsö, which was just about within range of an attack from Britain, provided the Lancasters were modified.

More powerful Rolls-Royce Merlin 24 engines were taken from other Bomber Command aircraft, the heavy armour-plating was stripped from the Lancasters chosen for the attack, the mid-upper gun turrets were removed, and overload petrol tanks originally designed for Wellingtons were retrieved from Bomber Command dumps and installed.

The attack aircraft were despatched to Lossiemouth, the closest station to Tromsö, to await good weather. However, it looked as though decent conditions would never arrive, and so on 28 October 1944, the Lancasters of 617 and 9 Squadrons attacked again, but cloud cover protected the ship.

Finally, on 13 November, 617 Squadron took off again. This time they could see the target clearly (the Germans had not had the time at Tromsö to put in place the smoke-making machinery they had used at Altenfjord). One bomb struck the *Tirpitz* amidships and another abaft the main gun turret. Damage was extensive, and after about twenty minutes an enormous explosion ripped a hole 120 feet long in the battleship's port side. She turned turtle and her superstructure became embedded in the sand. This was the end of a battleship which had won victories for four years just by her existence.

Incredibly, there were those who seemed to find it impossible to give credit to Wallis's TALLBOY. Wallis wrote to Lennox Boyd:

One cannot help feeling amused by the efforts of the sundry experts to prove that the ship would have been much more easily sunk by half a dozen 2,000-lb bombs containing 170 lbs of charge each. They give the impression of feeling that we have played a dirty trick on them, and that TALLBOY has no business to sink the ship, principally for the reason that they said it couldn't.

I think the most effective reply is that if the ship was so easily sinkable with 2,000-lb bombs which have been in existence for some time, why was she not sunk a long time ago?

Meanwhile, Wallis's TALLBOYS were being used effectively in support of the US and British armies. Between the second and third attacks on the *Tirpitz*, 617 Squadron was ordered south from Lossiemouth and attacked the Krebs Dam. The Americans were held up in the Belfort Gap between the Vosges and Jura mountains in northeast France near the German/Swiss border, and it was feared that when they broke out and attempted to cross the Rhine, the Germans would open the flood-gates of the Krebs Dam. The Allies decided therefore to open the gates themselves. However, the Lancasters were no longer fitted with the necessary equipment to launch Wallis's bouncing bombs, and the chances of a direct hit with TALLBOYS were small. After consultation with Wallis, it was decided to drop TALLBOYS with delayed fuses. These worked like a dream, and down went the Krebs Dam, so that the Rhine fell to a level that meant river barges well into Switzerland were left grounded in the mud.

Grand Slam, effectively the 10-ton bomb that Wallis had been so keen on ever since the beginning of the war, enjoyed only a short period of success as the war came to a conclusion.

It was dropped for the first time in an attack on the viaduct at Bielefeld in Germany by 617 Squadron, by this time under the command of Wing Commander J.E. Fauquier, on 14 March 1945, less than two months before VE Day on 8 May. This attack was hugely successful, as one of the Grand Slam bombs demolished seven spans of the double concrete viaduct.

Both TALLBOY and Grand Slam bombs were dropped in the final weeks of the war, helping to reduce German industrial production drastically as the whole Nazi regime collapsed. But by VE Day, Wallis had moved on in his mind to his next great project. On that memorable day, he wrote in his diary: 'Work on supersonics.'

And a week after the US Air Force dropped the atomic bomb on Hiroshima, a bomb which made even TALLBOY and Grand Slam look puny, he again wrote: 'Supersonic work.'

CHAPTER SEVEN
AFTER THE WAR

WILD GOOSE

In 1945, Wallis was made a Fellow of the Royal Society and was awarded the Ewing Medal. However, he was still not honoured with a knighthood. Wallis himself thought that it was because of the politics at his employers, Vickers, and he wrote to his colleague Trevor Westbrook:

> It was very nice of you to expect to see a Knighthood for me, but I have been informed on very high authority that this was twice turned down by Sir Charles Craven and until some change of policy is adopted by our directors I do not think that you will find that any technical official will be permitted to receive a Knighthood until the whole hierarchy of directors has been suitably rewarded ... Now that I have got the FRS [Fellow of the Royal Society] I do not really care what happens, but I would not change that for a dukedom and it is the only scientific distinction in the world which is really worth having and which cannot be bought either by fear or favour.

Wallis's reputation was such that, by the end of the war, Sir Hew Kilner put him at the head of the research department formed at Vickers, Weybridge. Wallis's brief was to involve himself in any work that interested him. As J.D. Scott put it in his history of Vickers:

No terms of reference were laid down and no objectives were designated. Kilner did not know, at this stage, that Wallis's interest in long-range communication had led him to take an interest in developing aircraft with variable geometries; still less did he know that Wallis had already gone some way in design studies of an aircraft based upon this revolutionary principle. The design in which Wallis was interested was a 'wing-controlled aerodyne', in which the wings could be at different angles of incidence and azimuth to the fuselage, and his interest in such aircraft arose out of his experience in the design of airships. He was familiar with the fundamental work of the eminent mathematician Sir Horace Lamb, who had demonstrated that the only stable mode of progress for an ellipsoid was broadside on, since in any other mode of progress it developed a pitching moment, and he was well aware that the elements required for controlling this pitching moment in a conventional aircraft were responsible for about 20 per cent of drag and for 15 per cent of the total structure weight. If these elements could be eliminated the gain to flight would be immense. If control by movement of the wings could be substituted for them, the aircraft would become immensely more capable of undertaking mutually antagonistic tasks: for example, bearing off the ground a load of fuel, enabling it to fly at very high speeds over very great distances.

When Wallis did broach his plans to Kilner, Kilner proposed that an approach should be made to Sir Ben Lockspeiser, then chief scientist to the Ministry of Supply. Wallis's ideas were of great interest to the Ministry, and Lockspeiser invited him to develop them in a paper. This work took Wallis about a year, and when the paper was complete it was passed to a committee of the most distinguished aeronautical scientists in the country, and was very quickly given their preliminary blessing. The welcome was enthusiastic; Sir Henry Tizard thought that the new project might be, 'in the end, comparable to the introduction of radar'.

This is what Wallis himself said of the development he called 'Wild Goose':

Wild Goose is the name given to a new type of aerodyne in which Stability and Control are obtained by making use of the Pitching Moment characteristics of ichthyoid bodies, when flying at small angles of incidence to the prevalent air stream.

These characteristics are sensitive to the presence of protuberances on the forward part of the body; and can probably only be developed to the fullest possible extent when at least half the length of the body from bow to midships is entirely free from any alien change in shape.

27. Air Chief Marshal Sir Arthur 'Bomber' Harris looks tough, and he was tough. He needed to be, to withstand all the attempts to deflect him from what he believed to be the correct way to win the war. He gave most people a hard time, and Wallis was no exception. When Wallis was trying to convince him that his dambusting idea would work, Harris replied: 'This is tripe of the wildest description. There are so many ifs and buts that there is not the smallest chance of it working ... I don't believe a word of its supposed ballistics on the surface ... at all costs stop them putting aside Lancasters and reducing our bombing effect on this wild goose chase ... The war will be over before it works – and it never will.'

28. Harris planning the Dams Raid. In spite of Harris telling his aides that 'I am now prepared to bet that the Highball [he should have said Upkeep] is just about the maddest proposition as a weapon that we have yet come across', he was soon captivated by Wallis's idea. As well as authorising the necessary modifications to the Lancaster bombers which would carry the dambusting mines, he took great interest in the plans for the raid.

29. Air Marshal Arthur Tedder, Director General of Research and Development at the Air Ministry from 1938 until 1940, was a great supporter of Wallis and his ideas. When Tedder was appointed Air Commander in the Middle East, Wallis sorely missed that support.

30. TALLBOY – Wallis's 12,000-lb bomb was so dear to his heart that he always described it in capital letters. He had lobbied for its use since the early days of the war, but it was only after the success of the Dams Raid that he was authorised to proceed with its development. TALLBOY combined great penetrative power – largely thanks to its streamlined shape, its 11-foot-long tail and its fins which produced spin – with tremendous blast effect. It was used with great effect against the V-weapon installations including Peenemunde, Siracourt, Watten and Wizernes in 1944, and was also the bomb used to sink the German battleship *Tirpitz*.

31. Duncan Sandys with Lieutenant General H.E. Franklyn (in uniform). Sandys fought with the British Expeditionary Force in Norway, and was wounded in action. The son-in-law of the Prime Minister, Winston Churchill, he was given a ministerial post in the wartime coalition government and was Chairman of the War Cabinet Committee for defence against Germany's V-weapons. After the war he was appointed Minister for Defence, and in 1957 produced the Defence White Paper which favoured missile technology over the use of manned fighter aircraft.

32 and 33. Grand Slam. The next stop from Wallis's 12,000-lb TALLBOY was his 22,000-lb bomb, Grand Slam (above and top right). With a length of 35 feet 5 inches, a diameter of 3 feet 10 inches and a tail of 13 feet 6 inches, Grand Slam was a truly scaled-up version of TALLBOY, combining its streamlined penetration with its huge blast effect.

34. Grand Slam was dropped for the first time on the viaduct at Bielefeld by 617 Squadron on 14 March 1945, demolishing seven spans of the double concrete structure. Manufactured at Vickers' works on the River Don at Sheffield, only about 35 were made, and were dropped in the final two months of the war.

35. Barnes Wallis with his close friend Mutt Summers (left) and General James Doolittle (in uniform). Summers was chief test pilot for Vickers for 21 years from 1929 to 1950, flying no fewer than 360 different types of aircraft. In 43 cases it was the aircraft's first, and therefore most dangerous, flight. He worked closely with Wallis on test-runs for the Dams Raid. Doolittle will be forever famous for the 'Doolittle Raid' on Japan immediately after their attack on Pearl Harbor. He came to Europe in January 1944 to command the US 15th Air Force.

He felt that research should be carried out thoroughly on the shape of the bodies that they wanted to project at high speed. And it was not only bodies flying through the air for which the research would be relevant. Wallis wrote:

> As the mathematical treatment of such shapes when moving in a continuous fluid is identical for air and water, it was suggested that the work to be undertaken on aerodynamic grounds would be equally applicable to submarine bodies.

FUTURE DEVELOPMENT OF AIR POWER

Wallis's view of the world air situation and its future was set out in a lecture he gave in December 1948 on the 'Future Development of Air-Power'. In it, he said about long-range aircraft:

> To help in defining the performance of long-range aircraft we may begin by assuming a reasonable war hypothesis, namely: that Russian aggression has at last led to a state of open warfare, which, preceded as it will have been by some years of cold war may have led if not to the actual occupation, then at least to the terrified neutrality not only of the whole European continent from France and the Netherlands in the west to Romania and Greece in the east but to Burma and China in the Far East as well. In formulating our technical requirements it would surely be unwise to rely on any more favourable conditions to the Eastward than those that actually

147

existed for the greater part of the last war, with the added handicap that the whole of Northern Africa, both shores of the Red Sea, the great Indian Continent and Ceylon, will all, at the best be neutral, and at the worst may be in Russian occupation.

Thus, between ourselves and the Australian Continent there may be no intermediate stopping place at which British aircraft can either re-fuel or re-arm ... We must therefore consider flying *non-stop* between England and Australia.

He went on to say:

It is becoming increasingly evident that the anatomical plan of conventional aeroplanes is not well-adapted for speeds approaching the speed of sound, neither does it lend itself to the great increase in size which the demand for long range and large pay-load is compelling designers, who work in an unsuitable technique, to adopt; lateral control by means of the conventional aileron is already giving trouble ... Even at subsonic speeds the increase in tail volume rendered necessary by multiple engine installations involves fitting a tail the drag of which may be as much as 20 per cent of the total profile drag of the aircraft, the weight thereof lying between 3 and 5 per cent of the all-up weight of the complete aeroplane.

There are good reasons, therefore, for concluding that the time is ripe for a big change in the anatomy of aircraft, and the object of the present paper is twofold; firstly, to suggest that logical advance lies in *the application of the aerodynamic character-*

istics of solids to the stabilisation and control of aerodynes with an accompanying revolutionary change in anatomy and technique; and secondly to show as far as present knowledge and the author's ability allow, that this proposal is practicable and will remove the difficulties with which we are now faced.

The bare anatomical form which evolves from the first suggestion comprises only three organs, namely a body and two wings. The wings may be moved at will relative to the body on which they are mounted, the movement of the wings relative to the body being used to control the motion of the aerodyne in flights; while body and wings acting in conjunction render it stable. It seems preferable, therefore, to refer to the resulting flying machine as an aerodyne rather than an aeroplane, since the latter term has come to be associated with flying machines the wings of which are fixed either to the body or to each other; and as aerodyne itself is a broad generic term it is convenient to distinguish this new species of the genus as a 'wing-controlled aerodyne' or for short, WCA.

Wallis was flying in the face of convention, if you will excuse the expression. Harking back to his airship days, he wanted to abolish both the tail and the aileron, thereby reducing both profile drag and all-up weight. However, this was not a development of the aeroplane but rather a new type of aerial vehicle and, as was often the case with Wallis's developments, was going to require massive research and development to prove its efficacy.

BRITAIN'S DEFENCE POLICY

In terms of defence priorities after the war, Britain, having first proposed a joint effort with the United States on nuclear weapon development and been largely rebuffed, decided to go it alone. Ernest Bevin, the determined Foreign Secretary, expressed his views succinctly, declaring that he wanted the bomb 'with a bloody Union Jack on it', and that's how Britain's nuclear programme proceeded. However, it was expensive and put pressure on other weapon developments.

Further financial pressure was exerted by Britain's decision to support the USA in the Korean war in 1950. The rearmament budget for 1951–4 was no less than £4.7 billion (about £120 billion in today's money). The debate about expenditure on conventional defence weapons continued throughout the 1950s. When Winston Churchill returned as Prime Minister in 1951, he upheld the view that Britain could not maintain its position as a world power without the most up-to-date weapons.

The debacle of the Suez invasion in 1956 and pressure on sterling meant cuts in the defence budget. The Joint Planning Staff strongly recommended that Britain cut back on her commitments around the world. The Army's contribution to NATO should be reduced, and the RAF would be concentrated in the British Isles – although a force of four bomber squadrons, with the capability of dropping nuclear bombs, would be stationed in the Middle East. Those in National Service were cut back sharply, and National Service was dropped altogether at the end of the 1950s. The result of all these suggestions was a Defence White Paper in 1957 which became known as the Sandys White Paper, after Duncan Sandys who was the Minister for Defence at the time.

Sandys was also the son-in-law of Winston Churchill, and was therefore in a strong position to push through the cuts in defence expenditure that were becoming increasingly necessary. As Michael Dockrill pointed out in his book, *British Defence Since 1945*:

> Britain's possession of a growing nuclear arsenal provided Sandys with a convenient rationale for cuts which the government would have been required to introduce for financial reasons.

The new Prime Minister, Harold Macmillan, increased Sandys's powers by creating a Defence Board which consisted of three service Ministers, the Chiefs of Staff, the Chief of the Defence Staff, the Chief Scientific Adviser to the Ministry of Defence, and the Permanent Under-Secretary at the Ministry, chaired by the Minister for Defence, and which was intended to co-ordinate defence and service policies.

Sandys's White Paper was particularly severe on the Army, but the RAF did not escape unscathed, and the implications for aircraft development were far-reaching. The first entry for Duncan Sandys on the Google search-engine on the internet reads:

> Duncan Sandys (pronounced 'sands') is quite poss-ibly the most vilified person in the history of British aviation. He is seen by most aviation writers and enthusiasts as the man who destroyed the British aircraft industry.

151

This is unfair. The truth was that Britain's economic circumstances did not allow her to continue as though she was one of the world's superpowers, spending money on all three sections of the armed forces as though it was her job to police the world.

As far as Barnes Wallis was concerned, this was the second time that Duncan Sandys had been instrumental in decisions that affected projects in which he was involved. In 1943, as we have seen, Sandys had been appointed chairman of the Cabinet committee to investigate the threat posed by German rocket weapons. In the mid-1950s, as Secretary of State for Defence in the Macmillan government, he presided over one of the darkest periods in British aviation. He proclaimed that the era of manned aircraft was over, and that rockets and missiles were the way forward. In the 1957 defence White Paper (a report outlining government policy), he cancelled all manned combat aircraft projects in the pipeline. The exceptions were the Lightning, which was about to enter service, and the replacement for the Canberra bomber, ultimately the TSR2. These cancelled projects included the Saro 177 rocket/turbojet interceptor, the Hawker P1121 multi-role aircraft and the Avro 730 reconnaissance bomber. Some of the finance freed up by cancelling these projects was transferred to rocket projects such as the Blue Streak. Having decimated the British aviation industry, he laid the foundations of the process that saw the many individual aircraft-builders merged into two major companies, Hawker Siddeley and the British Aircraft Corporation.

As Michael Dockrill points out, much of Sandys's plan proved impossible to carry through:

Nuclear deterrence was regarded as a means of obtaining a capability for defence and retaliation on the cheap, while Britain's insistence on remaining an independent nuclear power compensated to some extent for the loss of her *amour propre* in November 1956. The RAF believed that it would provide a useful adjunct to the US Strategic Air Command in the event of a nuclear war with the Soviet Union: indeed, the RAF would be able to bomb targets in the USSR which the United States did not feel to be essential to their plans while, if the United States, faced after 1960 with a Soviet retaliatory capability, refused to come to the assistance of Western Europe in an emergency for fear that her towns and cities would then come under attack, Britain would have the ability to act independently against the Soviet Union. Consideration was given at this time to sending nuclear weapons to Singapore for SEATO [South East Asia Treaty Organisation] purposes and to stockpile them in Cyprus for the defence of the CENTO [Central Treaty Organisation] areas.

None of these calculations was fulfilled. Nuclear deterrence was destined to become a commitment of ever increasing expense as new and more sophisticated missile systems were developed more frequently. It soon became beyond Britain's financial and technological capability to produce these weapons herself and she was forced after 1960 to buy them more cheaply from the United States.

The cuts that Sandys proposed were intended to reduce defence expenditure from 10 per cent of gross national product to 7 per cent. In fact, as Kenneth O. Morgan says in *The People's Peace*:

> Overall, defence expenditure in 1963 was running at £1,721m a year, almost a tenth of the gross national product.

In spite of the cuts, there were still several expensive programmes to be financed: the tactical strike and recon-naissance aircraft TSR2, Blue Steel, Thunderbird 2 and Sea Slug 2. As Solly Zuckerman, a successful business-man and adviser to the government, pointed out in his autobiography, *Monkeys, Men and Missiles*:

> It was as plain to me as it was to Harold Watkinson, my Minister, that the total defence R&D pro-gramme was hopelessly overloaded, and that a few major items were responsible for most of the strain. When the war ended in 1945, the Ministry of Supply was promoting scores of weapon-development proj-ects, many of which were still in being in 1960. The decision that Britain should become an independent nuclear power was taken in January 1947, with our first bomb being tested in 1952, and ... with the RAF having begun to plan for an operational nuclear bomber force as early as 1946. The Valiant and the Vulcan entered squadron service in 1955 and 1957 respectively, and the Victor was adapted as an air-to-air refuelling tanker. The Vulcan was still flying in 1982, when it was used during the Falklands war. In addition, a medium bomber, the Canberra, was also coming into service at the start

of the fifties, and four fighters, which were later cancelled, were in various stages of development. There were other important aviation projects in the pipeline. The Royal Navy was developing its own fighter-bomber, the Buccaneer. The RAF was designing the TSR2 as a replacement for the sub-sonic Canberra which, although due to be withdrawn in 1965, was still operational in 1985. There was the P1127, a vertical take-off ground support machine, and a military transport, the HS681. Finally, there was the supersonic Concorde. The industry was also producing subsonic civil aircraft, of which the Viscount, a propeller-driven machine, was outstand-ingly successful, in contrast to the Comet, Britain's first jet passenger-aircraft.

The Services had clearly been operating as though the country could afford almost anything. The reality was utterly different. Defence had to be fitted into a new set of national priorities.

ELATION AND DESPAIR

Wallis's old friend, F.W. Winterbotham, arranged for him to meet Whitney Straight, the Managing Director of BOAC (British Overseas Airways Corporation), while Straight was on holiday at Taormina in Sicily. Straight was American but had spent a great deal of his time, and been partly educated, in England. He had been an enthusiastic racing motorist, and had moved into civil aviation and on into the Royal Air Force. By the end of the war he was a Group Captain and aide-de-camp to the King. Such a person would appeal to Wallis, but Wallis was nevertheless concerned that Straight and what he described as 'his so-called experts' might not understand 'the revolution that I can produce in air transport'.

Nevertheless, he did his best to convince Straight. Wallis wrote to his wife Molly:

> Imagine us sitting after dinner at his hotel on a terrace about 1,000 feet above the bay, with the great bulk of Etna outlined against the velvet blue of the western sky, while the precipitous face of the bay up which we climbed was picked out in fairy-lights winking from the white masses of the hillside villas glowing coldly in the light of the moon at the full; and all the while me, lecturing hard on future developments of aircraft, taking sips at intervals from a glass of Italian liqueur, and doubling my optimism at every sip!

Straight seemed to be impressed, and promised to talk to Tedder, by this time Chief of the Air Staff. The hope was that BOAC and the RAF could develop Wild Goose together. After three weeks, Wallis returned home to his beloved Molly in high spirits. Unfortunately, his optimism was misplaced. Within four years, all the supporters of the project – Lockspeiser, Tizard, Tedder and Straight – had moved on from the positions where they could help Wallis.

Wallis turned to the Americans, the only ones in the late 1940s with any money, and he went there in 1948. He returned empty-handed to continue his research and development. By 1949 he had proved, at least to himself, with hundreds of calculations and with scale-model planes, that his theories were correct. However, Wallis knew that scale-models were just the beginning; what he really needed was the money to build a full-scale model.

Wallis was never the most patient of men, but now he refused to contemplate risking a test pilot's life by sending him off in a manned model. Jeffrey Quill, his test pilot colleague from the 1930s, begged to be allowed to try, but Wallis refused. In spite of protests, Wallis persisted with testing unmanned models, launching them from a power-driven trolley. The first Wild Goose reared up on take-off, stalled and crashed. The next put her nose down and crashed straight into the ground.

During the cold winter months of 1950, Wallis persisted with tests at the National Aeronautical Establishment at Thurleigh near Bedford. He and his assistants camped there in huts, built not in the Second World War but during the First. By the summer of 1951, Wild Goose was at last ready for more expansive trials, and the team moved to Predannack aerodrome near Lizard in Cornwall. Trials continued both here and at Weybridge. Finally, in April 1952 there came a vital test. This is how Jack Morpurgo described it:

Now he could only watch – and pray.

The seconds ticked on like the days of eternity. Suddenly the jets fired. Wild Goose hustled down the track, leaped into the air and flew magnificently. At the first touch from Nash's controls [Nash was the pilot controlling Wild Goose from the ground] she turned right and for three-quarters of a circuit she answered every touch.

Wallis had drilled himself for years to maintain

calm in the critical moments of scientific experiment. But the exhilaration of this stupendous achievement destroyed his practised calm. He found himself shouting a delighted running commentary to the air, to the gorse bushes and to his one companion.

Then, with success complete, unnecessary disaster followed. Nash must have decided to bring the plane down. He was flying her at only a few feet above the ground at a speed of 150 mph. Deceived by the lack of perspective in a flat countryside he did not appreciate the closeness of some of the aerodrome buildings. Wild Goose hurtled within a few feet of the fire-engine standing close to the runway and shattered her beauty against a concrete shed.

Wallis cared nothing for the crash. This was his moment of triumph.

He wrote to Molly and compared his achievement with that of the Wright brothers:

The greatest contribution they made to the art of flying was ... lateral control, brought about by means of the aileron – a brilliant and novel invention, still 44 years later in universal use. And 44 years later gallant men's lives are still being lost because the behaviour of new aeroplanes is not exactly predictable as far as their controls are concerned. In particular as speeds become higher and higher the aileron type of lateral control becomes more and more dubious ... Now I have, in one great change, abolished the aileron and all other conventional controls as well, transforming the complexity of the type that has persisted for nearly half a century to the endearing simplicity of the Wild Goose – just one body and two wings and no other controls at all.

Surely now the board of Vickers would back him with the money he needed to take his development through the next phases, or if not Vickers alone, then backed by one governmental body or other. However, it was not to be. Doubts were expressed which, of course, Wallis took not for caution but for deliberate obstruction. As far as he was concerned, he would 'never again darken the doors of the Royal Aeronautical Establishment'; he had been 'insulted' by the Aerodynamics Division of the National Physical Laboratory, and the Civil Service was determined to 'do him down'.

As for Vickers, they asked George Edwards, chief aerodynamicist, to carry out a study for the development of a bomber to succeed the Valiant, built on Wild Goose principles. At the same time, they asked Wallis to provide irrefutable proof of the success of the Wild Goose trials within four weeks. Failure to do so would mean the withdrawal of their support for the Predannack experiments.

WILD GOOSE BECOMES SWALLOW

Goaded, Wallis as usual pushed himself harder than ever. Once again, Morpurgo described his position well:

Wallis's belief in Wild Goose had been unshakeable, but he had not achieved the high levels in the ratio of lift to drag for which he had hoped. Now, when he came to reassess the configuration, he envisaged a radical change in the cross-section of the fuselage, making the basic form that of the delta with an enlarged spine running down the middle. This revised geometry allowed him to pivot the wings at the base of the delta so that when in the fully swept-back position they formed a continuous line with the delta forebody. There remained only the problem of designing a joint that could be concealed entirely in the narrow depth of the delta at its base corners.

This modified concept was called Swallow rather than Wild Goose and, at least as far as Wallis was concerned, it was perfect and could have no competitor, in either subsonic or supersonic flight. And certainly the experts appointed by the Royal Aeronautical Establishment could find no fault – *in the theory*. The Ministry of Supply and the Air Staff seemed enthusiastic too, and talked of transferring the trials to Australia to speed up development.

In the meantime, experiments continued at Predannack, accompanied by moments of elation and despair. The first model turned turtle on its maiden flight, but Wallis persisted, and by 1955 had built an 8-foot-long rocket-propelled model which was fired on the artillery range at Larkhill on Salisbury Plain. Wallis was ecstatic. It worked aerodynamically at great height and at two-and-a-half times the speed of sound. But there were still problems with the structure of the forebody. Nevertheless, by the summer of 1956, most of the technical difficulties with Swallow had been overcome. As far as

Wallis was concerned, all that was needed now was for production at Weybridge to take over his theories and produce variable geometry aircraft for both military and civil use.

But it was not to be. At Vickers and at all the government agencies that had been involved, no one was prepared or able to raise the funds necessary for continued development. Still Wallis did not give up. He thought: 'Who *has* got the money?' The only answer was the Americans.

In a paper of April 1958 entitled 'The Swallow Project – A Variable Geometry Aircraft', aimed specifically at the (largely American-financed) Mutual Weapons Development Program (MWDP), Wallis wrote:

1) The Objects of the Project are threefold:

a) To develop an aircraft capable of attaining a very wide speed-band extending from moderate take-off and landing speeds to a cruising speed in the stratosphere about 1,430 knots.

b) With the same aircraft as in a) to attain a *very long still-air Range* e.g. from about 5,000 nm [nautical miles] to a maximum of about 10,000 nm, non-stop, without refuelling, using standard hydrocarbon fuels, and carrying a suitable military load.

c) To ensure that objectives a) and b) are secured with aircraft of the smallest possible size and all-up weight.

Method of Attaining the Objectives:
1) The a) Objective depends upon the successful development of variable-sweep wings, with engines pivotally mounted on them so as to keep the jet-axis

of the engines aligned with the free-stream independently of the sweep-angle of the wings.

2) The b) Objective depends upon the attainment
of a Lift/Drag ratio in supersonic flight of between
8 and 10. This involves the elimination, as far as
possible, of all surfaces which are inefficient pro-
ducers of lift but which add considerably to the drag
of an aircraft.

Collaboration with the MWDP was tried but ultimately
fell down because the association of the research with
defence requirements was in fact producing at NASA the
same attitude to the use of variable-sweep wings as at the
Royal Aeronautical Establishment. Official interest in
Wallis's imaginative Swallow concept for a highly efficient
long-range aircraft had rapidly declined. It was being
replaced by a desire to exploit variable wing-sweep as a
means of improving the low-speed characteristics of
otherwise conventional military aircraft operating in
various roles where, generally, economic use of fuel and
the attainment of very long range were of secondary
importance.

The failure of the cambered and twisted arrow wings
to produce the expected lift/drag ratio was due to shortcomings in the mathematical treatment of the wing
designs.

Collaboration with the Americans ceased early in 1960,
no MWDP funding of Swallow research ever having been
obtained. The Americans proceeded on their own course,
eventually producing the F-111 which bore little relation
to Swallow apart from the location of the wing pivots at the
ends of the base of the forewing, a feature which experi-

ence with Swallow had shown to be necessary in order to keep the movement of the centre of pressure in line with that of the centre of gravity as the afterwing was varied.

Major General Sir Charles Dunphie, as Managing Director (later Chairman) of Vickers, tried to evaluate the possible payback of all the money that the company had invested in Swallow. On 30 October 1958 he received the report he had commissioned, which said, *inter alia*:

> [A representative of Vickers] was surprised and pained [talking of a meeting with a Mr Cawood at the Air Ministry] to hear that Cawood gave us the impression that 'SWALLOW' was not the first priority research project for future aircraft in the eyes of the Ministry. [The representative] said that, in his view and in the view of many of those working around him, it was the first priority project and was much more attractive than the RAE supersonic liner project, although, of course, some of the RAE were bound to lean towards that, and it involves simpler engineering problems.

The report went on to say that it was felt vital that Vickers find out, without delay, whether the Air Ministry did feel that Swallow was top priority. For their part, the Ministry would want to know whether Vickers were giving it their full support. The report concluded:

> I therefore suggest that at the high level meeting you might:–
> 1. Demand to know whether 'SWALLOW' is top priority for research, and if not, why not.

2. Demand to know whether or not there is fundamentally a potential NATO Staff requirement for the 'SWALLOW' tactical aircraft, and if they don't know, whether the Staffs cannot be asked immediately.

3. Give some assurance of future V-A [Value-Added] backing in terms of design staff and money, on condition that the Ministry will provide favourable assurances in regard to (1) and (2) above.

4. If the answers to (1) and (2) are unfavourable, then I suggest you indicate that we shall be forced to surrender the project to the Americans, exacting such patent remuneration as we can.

In the end, the government, with many other technological demands on their plate – not least the Anglo-French Concorde which was running wildly over budget – decided that they could not subsidise Swallow further. The two key ministers, Duncan Sandys and Aubrey Jones, though 'personally well-disposed towards [Wallis]', according to Morpurgo, withdrew their backing, Sandys blaming the decision on the lack of support from Vickers.

In the *Sunday Times* on 19 January 1964, Tom Margerison wrote:

The Swallow project, like many of Barnes Wallis's ideas, was unfortunate. It was too bold, too novel, and the Government withdrew its support. In a way he is too bold, too academic. His method is to go back to first principles and to tackle every problem anew.

Wallis never gave up, as *The Engineer* made clear in an article in December 1971:

As Concorde receives official blessing from Government Ministers and mention is made of new Concorde derivatives, one of its chief critics – Sir Barnes Wallis – believes that hypersonic [hypersonic is defined as a velocity of 5 Mach, i.e. five times the speed of sound] – not supersonic – flight is the only answer to long-range high-speed travel between British territories without the need to touch down for refuelling.

Sir Barnes believes development need cost no more than £5 million which seems incredibly low compared with Concorde's £900 million.

Sir Barnes was convinced at first that variable geometry was the solution to hypersonic flight but when he came to apply it he found the aircraft would create a shockwave. Showing a slide of several current fighters, Dr Wallis said that they achieve supersonic flight by brute strength, for a few minutes only because of the fantastic fuel consumption. So difficult is the reduction of supersonic drag, while retaining a wing capable of reasonable take-offs and landings that Dr A.A. Griffith of Rolls-Royce had decided to throw the low speed wing overboard in favour of direct jet-lift engines. Great was his respect for his life-long friend but this was *not* the right solution because of the weight of fuel – particularly that required for landing after deceleration from supersonic flight and stopping in mid-air.

... The right way to achieve high supersonic L/D [lift/drag] is to use a slender delta, so that every part lies behind the high density air of the Mach cone, and to cut away the back side – which is almost useless for lift but [like] a flying telegraph pole because the angle of the sweep was so high.

How does Sir Barnes achieve Mach 5? He claims the aircraft designs itself because he has discovered that a wedge of equal lift to a cone has lower drag. Why not then he says, make a fuselage of a wedge shape from which it is possible to obtain lift at a lower drag – or more lift from the same drag?

But, he claims, aeronautical engineers have never had experience of producing rectangular section fuselages. Airship designers on the other hand, have. 'I am the only man left now in Europe who has designed, built and flown airships ... Because of this experience I can design rectangular fuselages based on airship practice and they are pressurised internally. And it would be possible to build a fuselage lighter than Concorde.'

TSR2

The TSR2 (T for 'tactical', S for 'strike', and R for 'reconnaissance') is important in the latter years of Wallis's career. The idea of designing the TSR2 as a swing-wing aircraft had been considered at the beginning of the project. However, this was formally rejected at an early stage, mainly because developing it in this form would have delayed the date when it would replace the Canberra bomber. In 1957, when TSR2 was formulated,

George (later Sir George) Edwards, by this time Managing Director of Vickers (soon to be part of the British Aircraft Corporation), felt that the swing-wing idea was premature. In spite of his best efforts, Wallis failed to persuade Vickers that the pivot mechanism which he had devised would be successful in the aircraft.

The TSR2 grew out of the decisions that followed the Sandys White Paper of 1957, which said that: 'Fighter aircraft will in due course be replaced by a ground-to-air guided missile system'; while British nuclear weapons were to be delivered for the present by 'manned bombers and ballistic rockets'. However, as the government had decided not to go on with the development of a supersonic manned bomber (it would not be able to see service for at least ten years), there was to be one more subsonic manned bomber, which would replace the Canberra. This aircraft was designated OR.339.

On 1 January 1959, contracts were awarded for the development of the OR.339, now called the TSR2, jointly to Vickers and English Electric.

By the early 1960s, as progress on the TSR2 slowed and costs escalated, Edwards began to wonder whether swing-wing was not the answer after all, especially as it became clear that the Americans were making faster progress with their variable geometry aircraft, the F-111. Nor did Wallis let him off the hook, never missing an opportunity to show his disdain for those still pursuing the fixed-wing philosophy.

By 1962, as Peter Thorneycroft became the ninth Minister for Defence in as many years, the problems of the TSR2 were becoming acute. No firm orders for the aircraft's production were placed, and the estimated production cost for each one was by this time over £2 million (over £40 million in today's money).

Solly Zuckerman in his advisory capacity was in a perfect position to see the problems. He wrote later:

TSR2, Thorneycroft said to me, was 'an albatross round our necks', and was seriously distorting the entire military procurement programme. I found it ironical that I once had to accompany him to a formal meeting with one of his Treasury ministerial colleagues to plead for the further funds which, if not forthcoming, meant cancellation.

I kept him informed ... about what I was learning about the progress of the R&D programme, and I warned that because of increasing technical demands and difficulties, it seemed highly improbable that the aircraft could come into squadron service before the end of the 1960s. I seem to remember that even the main avionics contractor, Ferranti, told us that the aircraft was becoming so complicated, with its forward- and sideways-looking radar and sensor/computer systems, that it would be impossible to fly it 'at tree height' in all weathers at near the speed of sound. On paper it all looked possible, but 'the state of the art' at the time made it improbable. I kept warning that even with its novel swing-wing, the F-111 looked more and more likely to emerge a less complicated and lighter form of fighter-bomber than the TSR2, with a far greater 'radius of action' – and sooner.

Another difficulty was that there were no buyers for the TSR2. The USA had its F-111 project. Our

European NATO partners were not in the market. In December 1963 Peter Thorneycroft, in order to spread the cost, had even proposed, but unsuccessfully, that a mixed-manned NATO squadron of TSR2s should be formed. The only likely buyer had been the Australian Air Force. George Edwards had visited Australia to try to make a sale, but some initial encouraging noises came to nothing. In the end, the Australians said they were going to buy the F-111.

In one of the many accounts that have been published about the cancellation of the TSR2, Stephen Hastings, in a book called *The Murder of the TSR2*, implies that Dickie Mountbatten and I deliberately discouraged the Australian Chief of Defence Staff from buying the TSR2, Dickie because he wanted to interest him in the Buccaneer, and I because I favoured 'buying American'. The implication is that, whatever its merits, we were both out to sabotage the TSR2. This was total nonsense. The Australian Air Staff could hardly have been ignorant of the controversies about the TSR2, or about how it compared technically and financially with the F-111. They probably viewed the TSR2, as did the American aircraft industry, as a symbol of an overloaded and non-competitive aerospace industry.

So Wallis did not have any involvement in the TSR2 and he had to watch in frustration as it absorbed more and more taxpayers' money which, as far as he was concerned, should have been spent on *his* projects. Zuckerman explained the background well in his autobiography:

Roy Jenkins, who was Minister for Aviation at the time, was the only personal friend I had in the new administration. But neither he, nor anyone else in the Government, could isolate the problem of the TSR2 from that of the aviation industry as a whole. Other projects, civil as well as military (and including Concorde), would also have to be pruned if something like a sensible aircraft programme were to remain. The unrealistic ambitions of the aircraft industry, so Roy informed Parliament, had resulted in a situation in which it had to be supported by a subsidy of, on average, £15 a year from every man, woman and child in the country. Nonetheless, Roy knew that drastic and immediate surgery was impossible. It was not only the RAF but also industry and the unions who were opposed. By April 1965, however, the Government decided that it could wait no longer, and the cancellation of TSR2 was announced. There was more to come.

Deprived of TSR2 the RAF felt naked, and the industry hailed the cancellation as a sentence of death – despite the fact that all concerned knew that the previous Conservative administration had had its worries about the project. The RAF, on the other hand, was temporarily silenced by an undertaking that the Government would purchase F-111s from America to fill the gap that the cancellation had made. This undertaking was never fulfilled. More than a decade was to pass before the Air Force got the plane it wanted – the Tornado, an aircraft which weighs about half what the TSR2 would have done.

36. Wallis at his desk after the war. In the background is a photograph of one of the dams breached in the famous Dams Raid. Wallis continued to work at his usual frenetic pace through the 1950s and 1960s, displaying his customary vision.

37, 38 and 39. Wallis with his wife Molly at White Hill House, Effing-ham. Molly Bloxham was the niece of the second wife of Wallis's father, Dr Charles Wallis. Barnes and Molly met when he was 35 and she was only 17, and their early courtship was carried on through the medium of him giving her lessons in mathematics by post. Molly's father initially opposed the relationship, but he gradually softened his stance and eventually the two were married in 1925, when he was 37 and she 20. They produced four children.

Wallis and Molly bought White Hill House in 1930, just as the world-wide Depression was beginning to hit the economy hard. When they saw the house, backing on to Effingham Golf Course in Surrey, it was only half-built. They inquired the price and were told £2,500 (about £137,500 in today's money). As it happened, Wallis was being paid £2,500 and he had savings of £2,500. He sold his shares and bought the house in Molly's name. Obviously anticipating his four children, he instructed the builders to turn the planned four bedrooms into seven.

40. Wallis in his office holding a model of Swallow (in the background is a photograph of the R100). By 1955, Wallis had built a rocket-propelled model eight feet long. This was fired at the artillery range at Larkhill on Salisbury Plain. It flew at great height and at 2½ Mach, and Wallis was ecstatic. But he was to be disappointed. Neither the British government nor Vickers would provide the funds for development and, in the end, nor would the Americans either.

CHAPTER EIGHT

WALLIS, THE MAN

CHRIST'S HOSPITAL AMONG THE BEST

This has been a book about Barnes Wallis's great achievements: the R100, the Wellesley, the Wellington, and the big bombs – Upkeep, TALLBOY, Grand Slam – and some of his less successful projects: Wild Goose and Swallow. He is, of course, best remembered for his bouncing bombs and the raid on the German dams. If you refer to bouncing bombs, everyone says: 'Oh yes, Barnes Wallis'; and if you say 'Barnes Wallis', everyone replies: 'Oh yes, the bouncing bomb.'

His place in the history of Britain in the 20th century is absolutely secure.

But what was Barnes Wallis like as a person? Like most people who achieve great feats, he was a complex character with many sides, not all of them easily likeable.

Again, like many other great men, Wallis did not appear to promise a long life of outstanding achievement as a child. He was given a good start by going to Christ's Hospital. He undoubtedly thought so himself, writing later:

The term 'Public School' is loosely applied to many schools, but when thinking essentially of qualities of personality and leadership it is to the *older* schools that we must look for the product that we need; and though clever scientists can devise means of *artificial ageing* by which the effects of many years can be brought about in a few days, the quick development of the age-long traditions of a mature Public School lies beyond man's ingenuity and Time alone can give perfection. Thus the number of Schools on which the country can call with certainty for her future leaders is strictly limited, and it becomes the more important that, as their numbers are small, each and every one should be used in this way to its utmost capacity. If age and tradition be the necessary qualifications of a school for creating leaders, then of them all Christ's Hospital should stand among the best.

Wallis credited the school with giving him a sense of self-reliance, independence and pride. We have already read of the beneficial influence of H.E. Armstrong and especially Chas. E. Browne. As we have seen, Wallis was one of five of Browne's pupils elected Fellows of the Royal Society. When Wallis left Christ's Hospital he was unsure what career to pursue but chose engineering, not because he felt passionate about it but because it seemed to offer the best prospect of employment close to where the family lived. In his social life as a young man he involved himself in chess, bridge and music, and he took dancing lessons, although he showed little interest in girls.

THE WOMEN IN HIS LIFE

According to Jack Morpurgo:

> Although he was suitably sociable at the tennis club or at dancing classes there is no evidence in his letters or in his memory that he ever sought the company of a girl. Not until the First World War (when he was close to thirty) did he take a girl to the theatre – and then only a cousin. Not until the same time was he kissed by a girl: his fiancée. As he grew older he developed a charm, an old-fashioned courteousness towards women which has aroused in them admiration, affection – even adoration – but he never attempted the offhandedness, the easy assumption of equality which is the hall-mark of the man who is comfortable and successful in the company of women.

Wallis was *very* close to his mother, and they worshipped each other. When she died he was distraught. He had just bought a sailing dinghy but could not bring himself to name it. He knew it was customary to give boats a girl's name, but the only one he could contemplate was Edith, his mother's name. However, that would only remind him of the sadness of her death.

The one person who captured Wallis's heart was Molly Bloxham, someone who perhaps reminded him of his mother. Molly, whose aunt became the second wife of Wallis's father, Dr Charles Wallis, met him when she was 17 and he was 35. Their friendship began when he was kind to her following a contemptuous remark from her father after she had suggested she might become a doctor. It flourished by letter when he returned to his studies at Chillon in Switzerland. As she was struggling with mathematics, he was able to give her what was effectively a correspondence course in the subject. Eventually Wallis proposed to her, though apparently they had never even kissed, and did not do so on this occasion either.

Molly may have been ecstatic, but her father was not. As Morpurgo makes clear, he made his views of such a relationship known to Wallis in no uncertain terms:

> That Christmas Day of 1922 Arthur Bloxham found it easy to exclude Barnes Wallis from the benefits of the Christmas spirit. No sooner was lunch over than he summoned Wallis to his study and there treated him to a diatribe against men who robbed cradles. Offering no concessions of kindliness or comprehension he refused to countenance any further association between his daughter 'and a man old enough to be her father'. Ordinarily hot-tempered and entirely capable of frenetic rows with men, equals or superiors, who questioned, undermined or otherwise endangered his professional achievements, in these entirely unfamiliar circumstances Wallis found himself dumb, incapable even of sensible thought.

During the first half of 1923, father Bloxham gradually softened his position and even allowed Wallis to take Molly to the theatre, provided he always took his sister as well. Their relationship strengthened, with Wallis writing to Molly almost every day, even when he was seeing her as well. During 1924, Bloxham softened further and conceded that if, after Molly had gone abroad for three months, they were still intent on becoming engaged, he would accept it. All went according to plan, and they eventually married on St George's Day 1925. She was 20, he was 37.

The marriage was always a happy one, though it required great tolerance and patience on Molly's part. Wallis, when obsessed with a project, would work at it oblivious of the normal conventions of telling her where he was, what time he would be home and so on. In the early years of their marriage, the obsession was the R100 airship. There were many ruined dinners and even lonely nights for Molly when Wallis never came home. Soon, fortunately, the first baby was on the way, and Barnes junior was born on 1 February 1926. He was soon followed by a daughter, Mary.

And how was Wallis with his children? According to Morpurgo, not very good:

> He was not, as a general rule, easy in the company of his own children, nor they with him; his own Victorian notions of discipline and his eternal pre-occupation with his work strained the relationships beyond the possibility of comfort. His affection he had lavished openly on his mother and on Molly but he seldom showed any warmth towards his children (so seldom that Mary was to say that she would have been amazed had he ever kissed her or held her on his knee).

MARIE STOPES CONNECTION

Mary was to be a catalyst for some of the more bizarre episodes in Wallis's private life. First there was the coincidence linking Mary's future husband with the Lancaster bomber, which carried Wallis's mines to the dams and later his big bombs to other targets.

The Lancaster was built by the company A.V. Roe, whose main factory was in Manchester. The firm had been founded by Alliott Verdon (known as 'A.V.') Roe in 1909. He was financed by his brother, Humphrey, from the proceeds from the family firm, Everard and Co., webbing manufacturers specialising in braces. Everard's best-known product was called Bullseye Braces, and when it was known that A.V. Roe's biplanes were financed by Humphrey Roe, the stock joke was that they were kept up by Bullseye Braces. In a financial sense, this was perfectly true. By the time the First World War broke out, Humphrey had invested £10,000 (£1 million in today's money) in the company.

The war brought strong growth for A.V. Roe. It was an Avro fighter that brought down the first Zeppelin over Britain, and it was Avros which attacked the Zeppelin sheds at Friedrichshaven. By the end of the war, the company had manufactured 10,000 aircraft and both Alliott and Humphrey were rich.

In early 1918, Humphrey met Marie Stopes, the pioneer of sex education. They fell in love, and even though Humphrey was engaged, he extricated himself and he and Marie were married on 7 May 1918. Marie herself had been married before but, incredibly, even after a marriage lasting five years, she was still a virgin. Her first child was stillborn but eventually a son, Harry, was born on 27 March 1924. The *Daily Sketch* wrote:

> Famous Advocate of Birth Control a Mother. Authoress and Linguist. Story of Romantic Marriage to Aircraft Pioneer.

Marie Stopes was an imperious, frightening woman (she had frightened her first husband into impotence). Her biographer, Ruth Hall, wrote:

> Marie was convinced that Harry Verdon Stopes-Roe was the most extraordinary child ever born to woman (she had many a wrangle with the aged Mrs Stopes as to which of them had produced the most beautiful baby). Most mothers think this about their children, of course, but Marie pursued the feeling to obsessional lengths. A month after Harry's birth, she wrote to Professor Wheeler, her former colleague in coal research, and Harry's godfather: 'I want to let you see Baby Harry, otherwise known as the infant Hercules, for he lifted his head and poked it around while lying on his "tummy" when only one day old, a feat which is only achievable, according to Truby King's standard work, by a child of two months old. He really is a remarkable baby.'

Her problems as a mother were rather different from those of the mothers she wrote for. Where, she complained, was she to find a cook good enough to make the kind of nourishing milk pudding suitable for her son? Where was there a nursemaid of sufficiently high standard to cope with such a paragon?

When Harry was just over a year old, Marie wrote to the nursing agency who supplied her with a constant stream of replacements. The latest, she informed the agency, had many admirable qualities, but 'I left her in sole charge for two weeks while I was away from home and parted with a blooming healthy baby to return to find a pale, ill child about whose condition I was so worried I had to take him at once to see a specialist.'

What is the relevance of all this to Barnes Wallis? In October 1935, Wallis's wife Molly took their eight-year-old daughter Mary to a children's party. At the party there was a young, beautiful, long-haired child wearing a skirt. It was impossible to tell whether this person was a boy or a girl. It turned out to be a boy, the eleven-year-old Harry Stopes-Roe. Apparently Marie Stopes did not believe in the 'ugly and heating-in-the-wrong-place garments which most men are condemned to wear'. Her son's genitals should develop free of any such restrictions. According to Jack Morpurgo: 'Later Molly came to know that for the same reason Harry was forbidden a bicycle.'

When Molly heard that Marie Stopes herself was coming to the party she was determined to meet her, as she had long admired her work. Wallis had read Stopes's book *Married Love*, and had lent it to Molly when they became engaged. As it happened, when Stopes arrived Mary and Harry were dancing together. However, this did not impress Stopes, and she snubbed Molly. But Molly Wallis was a strong character herself and refused to be treated like this. Eventually, she arranged a meeting between Harry and her son. Indeed, young Wallis, but not poor Mary, was invited to the impressive Stopes-Roe mansion, Norbury Park.

This hospitality had to be repaid, and Marie Stopes was invited back to Effingham. It was not a happy occasion. Although Barnes Wallis had read *Married Love*, it was the only thing about Marie Stopes that he did admire. He thought her other books lightweight and her scientific claims pretentious. Wallis, however polite as a host he determined to be, could not contain himself at Stopes's arrogance and lack of real knowledge, especially when she started to give her opinions on aeronautics, a subject on which he was an expert and she was a complete ignoramus. Luckily, before a shouting match ensued they decided to play chess, but even here they could not agree. She wanted to play 'quick chess', in which no time was allowed for thought, a method that appalled Wallis as being entirely contrary to the spirit of the game. The final disaster came when Molly decided to breast-feed her younger son, Christopher. Surely Stopes would not disapprove of this. But she did.

Finally, Humphrey Roe arrived and took her away shouting as she left that she had let Wallis win only because she had to leave. They never spoke again.

MARRIAGE OF DAUGHTER MARY

As far as Marie Stopes was concerned, worse was to follow, in that her son Harry fell in love with Mary, who was not at all what Stopes had in mind as a suitable wife for him. According to Ruth Hall in her biography of Marie Stopes:

Her stipulations were that her putative daughter-in-law should be about twenty years of age, 'lovely and slender but with broad hip bones and broad breasts and broad brows, with eyes sweet and penetrating, deep and wise enough to see into the hearts of your babies and rear them with love.' Having met this ideal, child-rearing paragon, her son should ignore convention, waive the idea of 'settlements', and start an early marriage, using contraception before embarking on the domestic, child-rearing stage.

Unfortunately, Mary Wallis did not have deep, penetrating eyes, but was myopic and wore glasses. Hall wrote:

> Such a marriage, Marie thought, would be a eugenic disaster: were all her grandchildren to be born wearing spectacles?

As for Mary, she said a lot later of Marie Stopes:

> She terrified me. She had very piercing eyes – light hazel. Her hair was always untidy, she used to make her own clothes – cobble them up – fairly loosely corseted, to put it mildly. I suppose I was a mousy little thing – I should have stood up to her but I was too shy.

Notwithstanding these feelings of antipathy between the two families, Harry and Mary became engaged in October 1947. This did not stop Marie Stopes from crossing all the Wallises off the invitation list to her Christmas party at Norbury Park. Harry showed politeness by helping with the preparation, and then a new-found independent spirit by walking out of the back door as the guests came through the front door.

In an attempt to prevent the marriage, Marie Stopes wrote to Barnes Wallis, sending a carbon copy to Mary:

Dear Mr Wallis
I am greatly distressed by the news from Harry this morning that ... he has entered into a formal engagement with your daughter Mary ...

He has *no* prospects from me ... The income he has is small and is his own as his father and I gave it to him outright and with taxes and essential disbursements it amounts to no more than three hundred a year [about £9,000 in today's terms]. It is enough only to free his mind to devote it to his scientific work and develop unhampered his special scientific genius ...

... I may add that my extensive experience from my clinics makes my opinion on sex matters more than a personal one, and it is that Harry is physiologically ten years Mary's junior and they are sexually unsuited to each other and on Eugenic grounds I should advise against the marriage were they strangers to me ... Your precipitation of events is a tragedy to all, and the engagement a profound blow to my own happiness and our hopes for Harry's future.

As it happened, Wallis did not approve of the marriage either. He found Harry a little wild and unconventional.

However, by this time he was automatically going to take the opposite line to Marie Stopes. He wrote back:

> Harry is still desperately in love with Mary. Personally, I don't think it is much good opposing it and that the more we do the more awkward the position will be if he does finally do what he wants and marries her, for then we shall have to completely change our conduct towards her. It is all a puzzle …

This was fairly mild from the easily aroused Wallis, but he was not so docile when Marie Stopes suggested that a holiday in Europe had been arranged specifically for Mary to entrap Harry. Wallis threatened to sue Marie Stopes for slander. Finally, the marriage took place. Marie Stopes did not attend, though her long-estranged husband, Humphrey Verdon-Roe, did.

WALLIS AT WAR

It was during the First World War that an affliction that Wallis suffered through most of his life, migraines, began to affect him regularly. These could, on occasion, be so bad that they brought on bouts of depression, and when that happened Wallis became oblivious to other people's feelings. He suffered one such bout as 1919 turned into 1920 and the post-war slump took hold. His colleagues, as well as the directors, at Vickers tried to be sympathetic but Wallis brushed this aside, lecturing them and writing long letters on how they should reorganise the company.

As we have seen, Wallis had already shown signs of impatience when he had been thwarted in his ambitions. This trait became more marked under the pressures and urgencies of war. Again, Morpurgo put his finger on it:

His failure to walk the paths of persuasion step by step; his persistence in confusing some interest in his thesis with total acceptance, bemused his friends and angered even the most powerful among those prepared to become his allies.

As we have seen, his impatience led him to do something which, in retrospect, could have landed him in serious trouble with those responsible for the nation's security. He circulated his paper, 'A Note on a Method of Attacking the Axis Powers', to no fewer than 100 people, four of them in the still-neutral United States.

Occasionally, the patience of some of those above him snapped. Sir Charles Craven, the Chairman of Vickers, lost his temper with Wallis over the development of the Dams Raid bombs and, even as late as early 1943, ordered him to stop work on them.

Once the Dams Raid had been successfully carried out, Wallis's impatience with bureaucrats was reined back, although it flared again in his frustrating post-war dealings with them when he was working on Wild Goose and Swallow. Wallis could be inspirational to many, but he often managed to offend those who could prove useful to him. For example, Sir Solly Zuckerman, who was on the Advisory Council on Scientific Policy in the 1950s and early 1960s, told this anecdote in his autobiography, *Monkeys, Men and Missiles*:

A year later I was again at Manby, as one of a party of 'eminent scientists' who were being given a tour of a number of RAF establishments. Barnes Wallis was also a member of the group and, on the day we arrived, he invited me to go walking with him. Even though it was drizzling, I said yes, looking forward to a talk with the great man. We set off at a brisk pace, but after a few minutes he said that he never talked when on a walk. I kept up with him for about a quarter of a mile, and then turned back to the warmth of the mess building, leaving him to disappear into the mist. Wallis was an extraordinarily single-minded man.

As he grew older (by the 1950s he was in his 70s) Wallis became, if possible, more obsessive – note his obstinacy over flying Wild Goose and Swallow without testing with a pilot – and even more inclined to feel that people were deliberately obstructing him. This is what Morpurgo had to say about Wallis's frustrations over the development of Swallow:

> Wallis had proved a theory, and now expected that others with greater authority and infinitely expand-able bank-balances would take his proof as cue to total support and future action. Forty years of experience had not taught him all that there was to know about the obduracy of ministries and great corporations. But his optimism was short-lived and soon he was back to finding an enemy behind every Whitehall door ... These were ordinary hard-working officials, fearful of making a mistake and

in effect powerless to risk the grand gesture that Wallis demanded. Their timidity he took for jealousy, even for hatred, their lack of immediate enthusiasm for deliberate obstructionism. Here they were once more, the spiritual heirs of the men who had set their silly pride to the destruction of the British rigid airship, who had opposed his big 'plane and his big bomb, who had tried to interfere in his private war with Germany, and as he came again to resent their blindness so did he betray himself into peevishness.

He wrote to Molly that he could sometimes be 'touchy' with people. We can guess that she saw that as something of an understatement. However, she could only admire her husband's devotion to achievement and the fact that he did not know how to give up and relax. He wrote to her when he was well into his 70s:

Yet I go on, always some New Thing springing up, full of promise, meeting or avoiding all the old difficulties, just as it seemed that at last I must admit defeat and retire, old, discredited and disillusioned ... but here I am just turned seventy three years of age, still working all the days of the week and still developing and inventing.

And finally, in 1968, he was at last offered a knighthood. He had always been scornful of one, saying that being a Fellow of the Royal Society was all he had ever wanted. Indeed, he told Morpurgo that a knighthood would reduce him to the level ... and there followed a list of those honoured. Nevertheless, he now accepted the honour with alacrity and pride, and enjoyed it for the last eleven years of his life. He died in 1979 and could look back on a hard-working, exciting life in which he made an outstanding contribution to his country.

BIBLIOGRAPHY

Aldous, Richard, and Sabine Lee (eds), *Harold Macmillan and Britain's World Role*, Macmillan, 1996

Andrews, Allen, *The Air Marshals*, Macdonald, 1970

Barnett, Correlli, *The Verdict of Peace*, Macmillan, 2001

Barrymore Halpenny, Bruce, *Action Stations 2: Military Airfields in Lincolnshire and the East Midlands*, Patrick Stephens, 1981

Baylis, John (ed.), *British Defence Policy in a Changing World Role*, Macmillan, 1996

Bennett, Tom, *617 Squadron*, Patrick Stephens, 1987

Bowman, Martin, *The Wellington: the Geodetic Giant*, Airlife, 1989

Bowyer, Chaz, *Tales from the Bombers*, William Kimber, 1985

Bowyer, Chaz, *Bomber Group at War*, Ian Allan, 1981

Bowyer, Chaz, *Wellington at War*, Ian Allan, 1982

Braddon, Russell, *Cheshire VC*, Evans Brothers, 1954

Brickhill, Paul, *The Dam Busters*, Pan Books, 1951

Brower, Charles F. (ed.), *World War II in Europe, The Final Year*, Macmillan, 1998

Burke, E., *Guy Gibson VC*, Arco, 1961

Calvocoressi, Peter, Guy Wint and John Pritchard, *Total War*, Allen Lane, 1972

Cheshire, Leonard, *Bomber Pilot*, Mayflower, 1975

Clark, Ronald W., *Tizard*, Methuen, 1965

Clouston, A.E., *The Dangerous Skies*, Cassell, 1954

Cooper, Alan, *The Men who Breached the Dams*, William Kimber, 1982

Cooper, Alan, *Beyond the Dams to the Tirpitz*, William Kimber, 1983

Delve, Ken, *Vickers-Armstrong Wellington*, Crowood, 1998

Dockrill, Michael, *British Defence since 1945*, Basil Blackwell, 1988

Galland, Adolph, *The First and Last*, Bantam Books, 1978

Gibson, Guy, VC, *Enemy Coast Ahead*, Michael Joseph, 1946

Grey, C.G.A., *History of the Air Ministry*, George Allen and Unwin, 1940

Harris, Sir Arthur, *Bomber Offensive*, Collins, 1947

Hastings, Max, *Bomber Command*, Michael Joseph, 1979

Hecks, Karl, *Bombing 1939–45*, Robert Hale, 1990

Hennessy, Peter, and Anthony Seldon (eds), *Ruling Performance: British Governments from Attlee to Thatcher*, Basil Blackwell, 1987

Higham, Robin, *Air Power*, Macdonald, 1972

Higham, Robin, *Britain's Imperial Air Routes 1918–1939*, G.T. Foulis, 1960

Higham, Robin, *The British Rigid Airships 1908–31*, G.T. Foulis, 1961

Irving, David, *Hitler's War*, Hodder and Stoughton, 1977

Irving, David, *The Rise and Fall of the Luftwaffe*, Weidenfeld and Nicolson, 1973

Jackson, A.J., *Avro Aircraft since 1908*, Putnam, 2000

Jackson, Robert, *Airships in Peace and War*, Cassell, 1971

Jacobs, Peter, *The Lancaster Story*, Arms and Armour Press, 1996

Lamb, Richard, *The Macmillan Years 1957–1963*, John Murray, 1995

Lawrence, W.J., *No. 5 Bomber Group RAF*, Faber and Faber, 1951

Longmate, Norman, *The Bombers*, Hutchinson, 1983

Meager, Captain George, *My Airship Flights 1915–30*, William Kimber, 1970

Messenger, Charles, *Bomber Harris and the Strategic Bombing Offensive 1939–45*, Arms and Armour Press, 1984

Morgan, Kenneth O., *The People's Peace: British History 1945–89*, Oxford University Press, 1990

Morpurgo, J.E., *Barnes Wallis*, Ian Allan, 1972

Neillands, Robin, *The Bomber War*, John Murray, 2001

Penrose, Harald, *British Aviation, The Adventuring Years*, Putnam, 1973

Penrose, Harald, *British Aviation, Widening Horizons*, HMSO, 1979

Penrose, Harald, *British Aviation, The Ominous Skies 1935–1939*, HMSO, 1980

Probert, Air Commodore Henry, *Bomber Harris*, Greenhill Books, 2001

Richards, Denis, *Portal of Hungerford*, Heinemann, 1977

Robertson, B., *Lancaster – The Story of a Famous Bomber*, Harleyford, 1965

Rumpf, H., *The Bombing of Germany*, Frederick Muller, 1961

Scott, J.D., *Vickers: A History*, Weidenfeld and Nicolson, 1962

Sebag-Montefiore, Simon, *Enigma: The Battle for the Code*, Phoenix, 2000

Shute, Nevil, *Slide Rule*, William Heinemann, 1954

Speer, Albert, *Inside the Third Reich*, Weidenfeld and Nicolson, 2003

Thetford, Owen, *Aircraft of the Royal Air Force since 1918*, Putnam, 1957

Verrier, Anthony, *The Bomber Offensive*, Batsford, 1968

Watson-Watt, Sir Robert, *Three Steps to Victory*, Odhams Press, 1957

Webster, Sir Charles, and Noble Frankland, *The Strategic Air Offensive Against Germany, 1939–45*, Stationery Office Books, 1961

Winterbotham, F.W., *Secret and Personal*, William Kimber, 1969

Zuckerman, Solly, *Monkeys, Men and Missiles*, Collins, 1988

PICTURE CREDITS

Photographs 1, 2, 3, 8, 12, 13, 14, 15, 16, 17, 18, 19, 20, 21, 22, 23, 24, 25, 26, 27, 28, 29, 30, 31, 32, 33 and 34 are reproduced by kind permission of the Imperial War Museum.

Photographs 4, 5, 6, 7, 9, 10, 11, 35, 36, 37, 38, 39 and 40 are reproduced by kind permission of the University Library, Cambridge.

INDEX